Overcoming the Exploitation of Passion in Videogame Labor

STUDIES IN NEW MEDIA

Series Editor: John Allen Hendricks, Stephen F. Austin State University

This series aims to advance the theoretical and practical understanding of the emergence, adoption, and influence of new technologies. It provides a venue to explore how new media technologies are changing the media landscape in the twenty-first century.

TITLES IN SERIES

Overcoming the Exploitation of Passion in Videogame Labor

Playing with Passion

Joshua Jackson

LEXINGTON BOOKS
Lanham • Boulder • New York • London

Published by Lexington Books
An imprint of The Rowman & Littlefield Publishing Group, Inc.
4501 Forbes Boulevard, Suite 200, Lanham, Maryland 20706
www.rowman.com
86-90 Paul Street, London EC2A 4NE, United Kingdom

British Library Cataloguing in Publication Information Available

Library of Congress Cataloging-in-Publication Data Available

ISBN 978-1-66691-525-9 (cloth) | ISBN 978-1-66691-526-6 (ebook)

To my mom, dad, and stepmom and y'all's unwavering support. Sincerely: thank you.

Contents

Acknowledgments

I want to thank all of my informants for this project. Without all of y'all's willingness to take a chance to talk to me, none of this would be possible. I am so thankful for the relationships I've been able to foster, the trust that y'all have placed in me, and y'all's belief in this project.

I especially want to thank Dr. Helen Burgess for allowing me the space to explore things that, otherwise, I never would have thought to explore. You set me on my current path, and you enabled me to talk about really exciting, difficult things in exciting, difficult ways.

I want to thank Dr. Nick Taylor, Dr. Andrew Johnston, Dr. Stacey Pigg, and Dr. Anastasia Salter for all pushing me, giving me indispensable advice and viewpoints, and for bearing with me while I worked through some of the rigor that I wasn't expecting to take on.

Finally, I want to thank my friends who have listened to me, supported me, and made my life easier while I worked on this. Sylvester and Kyle (and Dunbar, my precious son); John, Patch, Conner and Lisa, Karol, Ben, Little Rob, and Kuma (my other precious son); courtney coles, whose art now graces my home *and* my freaking book's! COVER!; Cristen; Sarah and Max; and Brianna. I love you all and I'm very thankful for y'all's patience and grace.

Introduction

The Road to Hell Is Paved with Good Intentions

ROADMAPPING

Popular press coverage has laid bare what types of precarity videogame production workers face in the industry. Issues like crunch,[1] or extended periods of 60+ hour work weeks, opaque meritocratic advancement that favors certain people over others, and workplace culture fits that act as self-policing measures all characterize the types of precarity that videogame production workers face. 2018 work from Jason Schrier put forth a call for production workers to unionize alongside a 2019 *New York Times* piece that exposed the backbreaking labor that goes into making a videogame. James Batchelor's work for GamesIndustry.biz thoughtfully considers what the stakes are regarding the controversy around *Red Dead Redemption II*'s 100+ hour work weeks. Rebekah Valentine's work examines the disarray that the Electronic Software Association is in regarding how best to divorce themselves of a past that valorized overwork and burnout. In the past, videogame production has leveraged narratives such as of "gaming while you work," "doing what you're passionate about," and "working with like-minded people in like-minded environments." Ergin Bulut in "Glamor Above, Precarity Below" references images of "playing games at work or playing soccer in the fields of Electronic Arts" (197), which continue to be popular depictions of what it is like to work in videogame production. However, there are rather few examples that highlight the precarity that has taken place behind the scenes of videogame production. Until very recently, the perennial popular culture example of toxic working conditions in videogame production was Mike Capps' 2008 IGDA Leadership Forum comments. He stated that 60-hour work weeks were an expectation at the videogame production company Epic, and that Epic would not hire (or would soon after hiring, fire) workers who were not committed to spending this kind of time working on the games that they were making. Other exposés regarding precarity have fleshed out the contours of this problem. Ian William's 2013 Jacobin piece titled "You Can Sleep Here All Night" outlined how the videogame production industry subsists on exploitation of passion as a means of producing games with such quick turnaround. The "Rockstar Spouse" blog and "EA Spouse" blog are two early examples of people within the industry talking about what types of precarity they face and people they are close to face. Both of these blog posts came from spouses of videogame production workers. These blogs recount, for a non-videogame production audience, the tumult that production workers endure, and the toll it takes on their families. The questions remain, though: how do we keep account of these instances? How do we engage with them from a scholarly standpoint and a cultural standpoint? How do we come to understand the labor processes that occur in videogame production specifically, and media production widely that are producing the forms of precarity that this book will discuss? What can we do to address these concerns as scholars, as activists, and as consumers? How can we quantify immaterial labor against "hard" or "material" labor jobs when we talk about unionization and fair working rights? How can we understand the situated, embodied experiences of digital media production workers in such a way that it becomes real to us so their struggle doesn't remain abstracted? These questions characterize this book's main operating question: what does precarity look like in videogame production, and how does it function?

WHAT IS PRECARITY, WHY IS PRECARITY

For the purposes of this book, I am borrowing definitional work around what "precarity" manifests as or has been identified as in anthropology, science and technology studies, and English Language Teaching (ELT). Through a triangulation of culture, technology, and semiotic theory, it becomes clear how best to prepare for initial definitional work around what precarity looks like in videogame production. This definition will not stay static, though. Precarity is multifaceted and presents differently based on circumstance. Paul Walsh in "Precarity" defines precarity in ELT as a "condition resulting from an employment regime in which deregulated labor markets give rise to various types of insecure work; in which social protections are minimized; and in which the ability to plan a coherent future is compromised" (459). Walsh locates precarity in ELT as consisting of devaluation of labor of those teaching English in non-English speaking countries, and research and teaching material for ELT increasingly becoming beholden to capital generation and marketing imperatives (460). Clara Han in "Precarity, Precariousness, and Vulnerability" locates precarity in a similar way as Walsh in that precarity is labor- and capital-based, but Han draws upon Marx and Engels to understand precarity through a socioeconomic working lens. As states have withdrawn welfare and undergone austerity measures, encouraged the casualization of labor, and created informal and "gig" economies, there has coalesced a digital *lumpenproletariat*, or unanchored lower/unskilled class that is forced into intermittent labor to survive. As labor regimes have become more flexible, assaults on the "welfare state" continues, and the global economy becomes increasingly intertwined with the informational economy, Han locates precarity as meaning "those who would have expected long-term stable employment and the benefits of a welfare state [who today], instead, live through intermittent labor while thwarted in their aspirations for a 'good life' (Berlant 2011)" (335). Finally, Phoebe Moore in *The Quantified Self in Precarity* locates precarity, again, in terms of capital, but more as a bodily attribution: "[precarity] is the purest form of alienation where the worker loses all personal association with the labor she performs. She is disposed and location-less in her working life and all value is extracted from her in every aspect of life" (79). Moore locates precarity as something closer to what Lauren Berlant in *Cruel Optimism* characterizes the namesake of the book as: a search for the "good life," or stable, fulfilling work and grounded social attachments. Moore characterizes labor in an ever-growing informational economy as consisting of "constantly chasing the next 'gig'" (79), which renders spatial and temporal consistency in life out of reach for certain sectors of workers. Through these three pieces of definitional work in other fields, the idea of what *facilitates* precarity becomes easier to talk about, but the act of pinpointing what precarity *is* is still out of reach. We can ascertain that precarity has roots in, and is exacerbated by, neoliberalism, casualization of labor, and the strip-mining of worker protections and worker welfare, and we can ascertain that there are certain discursive situations in which these ingredients must be present for these attributions to be attached to a person. The informational economy, and derivative forms of "information" labor such as immaterial labor provides the circumstances necessary for precarity to manifest.

Mauricio Lazzarato in "Immaterial Labor" describes and contours forms of specifically nonphysical work that produces knowledge capital to the benefit *of* capitalism. Immaterial labor is often unremunerated and thought of as "just another job responsibility" in much of the tech sector, and especially in media production. Systems theory theorists Judith Innes and David Booher in "Consensus Building and Complex Adaptive Systems" and its derivative Communication Constitution of Organization, taken from *The Emergent Organization* by James Taylor and Elizabeth Van Every, both invite a positivist approach to dealing with interorganizational problems such as precarity by decentering the individual(s) experiencing precarity and instead inviting theorizing and action based on strategic alliance with other organizations. This means that, in lieu of situated protections for workers from systemic, organizational violence, organizations seek to align themselves with "initiatives" or "stances" against hot-button issues. This public-facing stance against, for example, overwork, garners positive public sentiment, which allows for capital generation to continue uninterrupted while also allowing organizations to continue allowing abuse to propagate.

What these and similar theoretical approaches elide, are the people that the precarity is affecting, and how those people came to be entangled in precarity in the first place. Within videogame production, more so than most other media production sectors, "passion" or "being a gamer" or "being hardcore" are traits that are fetishized in job ad material, interview material, and workplace culture. Cecilia D'Anastasio in "Inside the Culture of Sexism at Riot Games" provides a succinct example of this by talking about Riot Games' work culture. The hiring process described by her informants seemed contingent on them being "hardcore gamers": to the point that one informant told a story about a hiring manager blatantly harassing her about her characters' gear and raid progression in *World of Warcraft* to make her prove she was "hardcore" enough to work there. Aphra Kerr and John Kelleher in "The Recruitment of Passion and Community in the Service of Capital" describe the hiring process, job material, and job expectations of community managers in games and find that the word "passion" is one of the most used terms in the job ad material they examined. These jobs require people who are passionate about the games that they are supporting to undertake the huge emotional labor of supporting and being the face of an entire gaming community. Understanding how "passion" is operationalized to exploit workers and create precarity is the main conceptual backing of this book. But to understand why passion is such a powerful motivator, there is a deeper understanding that needs to be unpacked. The concept of "passion" often comes up as a footnote to some other identified problems when thinking about bodily entanglement with precarity. The passion, or lack thereof, that a person displays towards their workplace, work itself, bosses, peers, etc. is rarely, if ever, addressed in terms of its role in facilitating precarity.

Lauren Berlant's concept of cruel optimism, introduced in her 2012 book of the same name, is a way of understanding why people would put themselves in problematic, precarious, or exploitative situations willingly. Cruel optimism as a concept describes the proverbial carrot on a stick allure of a possibly toxic situation for a person: something that can be dangled in front of them to encourage them to work harder, do more, or push themselves in the hopes that their hard work will be recognized and they will be promoted or given more responsibilities. Berlant characterizes these attachments as "clusters of promises" (23) which can be examined to understand how attachments become "cruel." Attachments are not always straightforward. Why we become attached and transfixed by something is not always clear. Berlant argues that these attachments can be "incoherent or enigmatic . . . not as confirmation of our irrationality but as an explanation of our sense of *our endurance in the object*, insofar as proximity to the object means proximity to the cluster of things that the object promises, some of which may be clear to us and good for us whole others, not so much" (23). In videogame production, the ways in which these cruel optimistic attachments build and become recognized pathways to success, regardless of whether they valid pathways or not, can be seen in a number of instances. Williams in "You Can Sleep Here All Night" and Bulut in "Glamor Above, Precarity Below" talk about quality assurance workers working grueling hours in cramped rooms in the hopes of their work ethic being recognized. Bulut, in "Glamor Above, Precarity Below" also talks about videogame production workers working months of crunch in the hopes that the game sells well and they get rewarded with vested stock options or years-long payouts that will make the work feel "worth it." Robin Johnson in "Toward Greater Production Diversity" talks about contract-laborers constantly overworking in the hopes that they could be hired to be part of a core development team on some intellectual property (IP) or failing that, to make sure that they keep from being blacklisted in the production community. These problems are but observable instances of how cruel optimism manifests. The investments that go into building and maintaining these cruel optimistic situations are much deeper and more insidious than these isolated instances. Contract work, quality assurance work, and crunch are examples that assist in creating grounded understandings of why and how passion and cruel optimism come together in videogame production to be such a powerful tool for exploitation. To take these examples of work-related precarity further, though, and understand the infrastructural and capital-production-driven reasons for why they subsist in videogame production requires an understanding of many facets of videogame culture, game studies, and videogame production processes to get to the heart of the issue.

WHO ARE ALL THESE PEOPLE IN MY (VIDEOGAME PRODUCTION) HOUSE

The basis of this book is to understand, from a theoretical perspective and then from an embodied, personal perspective, how precarities manifest, and to provide some way forward for workers. Batchelor, Schrier, and Valentine's work talk about how precarity is manifesting in videogame production, but do not consider at any length the people who are suffering through these abuses.

The closest that these articles come is making sweeping generalizations about crunch and toxic workplace cultures as being bad for ALL production workers. Other popular culture work that I will engage with that talks about precarity in videogame production commit to the same method of generalization. Even the scholarly work that I engage with throughout this book that talks about videogame production does not do an adequate job of understanding the distinctly human element of videogame production. Often, production workers' thoughts or experiences are used to substantiate an author's claim about videogame production as a whole instead of attempting to engage with the embodied element of those stories.

Without the clarity and granularity that exploring individual, embodied experiences bring to light, generalizations made about videogame production will always miss the mark and will do no good in helping to bring about reform. At its core, this book is an intimately *human* endeavor; it is imperative to understand the stories, contexts, and experiences of the workers. In doing so, I hope to provide a platform by which I can elevate the stories and experiences being entrusted to me and make a case for why embodied knowledge is integral for collective action and unionization in videogame production. My ultimate hope is to parlay this understanding into lynch pins for success against union-busting efforts and continual government deregulation and erosion of state-sanctioned support. I also seek to explore the contours of what current videogame production "is" for workers, and what it could be. What would ethics of care look like in videogame production? How drastically would workplace cultures have to shift to accommodate and rehumanize workers seeking ethics of care? I aim to explore and create actionable interventions in both a scholarly and activist capacity that do not repeat the missteps that previous interventions into videogame production culture have made. The only way to accomplish these goals is to use methodologies that encourage intimate, embodied accounts of both the positive and negative experiences that workers have regarding precarity through talking to as many people working in the industry as possible and taking close notes regarding successful interventions such as we see with French videogame production union bodies. It is also important to understand that there is no possibility for a catch-all explanation or course of action that will protect and empower *all* videogame production workers. I argue that without intersectional, feminist, and queer interventions in videogame production, the importance of (re)centering people when talking about technical spaces would arguably not exist, and a book like this that seeks to foreground granular experience as a desired research output would not be possible. Understanding the granular, experiential knowledge of videogame production workers, the affects that surround their interpersonal interactions, and how best to talk through these things responsibly is difficult.

When the "face" of videogames is still far too often a white male face, representation is still quite a contentious issue. Even more so when considering who these representational bodies are forgetting. Todd Howard, Ion Hazzikostas, Jeramy Cooke, Randy Pitchford, Ed Boon, Peter Molyneux, Jeff Kaplan, John Smedley, Sam Houser, Rod Fergusson, Nolan Bushnell, Andy Gavin, Jason Rubin, Trip Hawkins, Doug Lowenstein, Peter Moore, Mike Morhaime, Scott Orr, Chris Weaver: each of these people have almost instant name recognition among people who are familiar with the videogame industry. They are presidents, founders, CEO/COOs, IP managers, community managers, or producers of some of the most well-known and well-received games, platforms, and innovations in videogaming history. Time and again, we see these familiar faces onstage at PAX, E3, Gamescon, BlizzCon, CES, GDC, and DreamHack,[2] presenting "the future" of their IP, company, or videogaming as a whole. The noticeable lack of women, queers, nonbinary and trans bodies, and bodies of color in positions where they are public figures is an ever-present reminder that diversity, and diversity initiatives in this industry still lack any sort of serious commitment to diversifying videogaming and videogame production. To truly promote diversity in this industry requires more than just "quick fixes" like including a token selection of diverse people in videogames or including queer romance options. Promoting and integrating diversity require systematically questioning why the videogame industry values men more than anyone else. Why men and why white people are seen as more valid and more expert than nonwhite and nonmen are. Why we overprivilege certain bodies with access to technics and tools that allow for creation while denying other bodies access at all based on biology. Creating a truly diverse, welcoming, and accepting videogame environment requires having some uncomfortable conversations about what an industry would look like that *doesn't* cater to primarily male people; one that doesn't conflate technical mastery with a set of genitals. What would an industry look like where people of color, queers, trans, and nonbinary bodies are in charge at all levels, including technical and ideological, and are not just "diversity hires" to fill check boxes? What would an industry look like where radical softness is valued over radical overwork—where human decency, empathy, and a pronounced "softness" towards peoples' bodies needing rest is valued over grinding people into dust? What would an industry look like where the people playing the games that are produced don't see the industry as a service industry, but as an industry where radically inventive ideas are valued? Some of these questions are outside of the scope of this book. But they are questions that have inspired this book and will continue to inspire my work for many years to come. These are questions that need answering, and this book will hopefully become a base camp of sorts where I can start climbing that metaphorical mountain. To start to traverse that mountain, it is necessary to examine theoretical understandings of "precarity" and draw from qualitative interviews to create a foundational definition of *precarities*. Instead of continuing to use "precarity" as a catch-all term to describe issues like trauma, vulnerability, and risk distribution, there needs to be a move towards describing workers' experiences as they are and what they evoke.

CHAPTER FLOW

In my first chapter, I go over some definitional work regarding precarity. This chapter starts by examining how "passion" is conceived of and operational-ized across a variety of business-oriented scholarship. This is done to lay the groundwork for understanding how passion is approached in videogame production specifically: how is passion being used to subjectivate workers into accepting toxic working conditions and workplace cultures? To under-stand this, the concept of immaterial labor must first be understood so that the specific types of precarity within immaterial labor can be examined. Once those understandings are established, it becomes possible to think through how, within videogame production, precarity manifests and who it affects. It becomes possible to intertwine the concept of cruel optimism with pas-sion as a way of understanding the complicity of one within the other. This approach allows for ways of thinking through what types of workers and what types of bodies are in danger of being further marginalized by the lack of clear understanding of unionization efforts and collective organization within videogame production. This chapter is acting as a literature review of what "precarity," "passion" and "cruel optimism" mean in highly specific and theoretical circumstances.

In my second chapter, I walk through the ways and means by which the societal expectations of how money flows from entity to entity and how cultural meaning markers are made (understood as the capitalist socius by Deleuze and Guattari (1983)) allows for certain forms of coerced expression, meaning-making, and identity-formation (understood as subjectivation by Deleuze and Guattari (1983)). This is especially prescient in videogame pro-duction where these forms of coercion ultimately end up as forms of precarity being operationalized and linked to units of surplus knowledge production. When we consider the ways and means by which the societal expectations that surround us, the cultural markers that influence us (and influence our spending habits!), and our conceptions of what very basic "work" is and how seemingly powerless we are to buck those trends, we are treated to a very bleak image of the productive needs of world capitalism to maintain auto-poiesis, or the perfect balance required to prop up this cycle of production. This includes the complete restructuration of emotion and operationalization of passion within videogame production in such a way that these measures become policing measures and metrics used to restrict the potential, multiplicative, in/organic bodily metamorphoses that *should* be present within a creative art such as videogame production. Ultimately, this chapter provides a messy way of understanding the cycles in which we find ourselves imbricated, but also provides a way of moving the conversation around the definitional work of "precarity" (discussed in the first chapter) towards something much more generative.

In my third chapter, I make tentative steps towards a theorization of *precarities*. The literature review that I did in the first chapter does a good job of outlining in very general terms what and where precarity can manifest and how that links to cruel optimism. But the term "precarity" does not do a good enough job of describing the experiences of my informants. Therefore, it is necessary to start to think beyond just a singular, all-encompassing understanding of the situations, affects, entanglements, and extenuating circumstances that surround and characterize my informants as just "precarity." The things that my informants talked about need to be understood on a more granular level than what classifying their experiences under "precarity" can provide. This chapter, instead, is interesting in taking formative steps towards understanding multiple, situated, embodied experiences as precari*ties*. This chapter looks at three themes that appeared across all my informants' stories, but varied wildly in scope, impact, and fallout. These themes are trauma, vulnerability, and risk. This chapter unpacks what these themes mean and how they collocated alongside, within, and outside a general understanding of singular precarity.

In my fourth chapter, I provide a future-facing look at what, hopefully, is next in the cyclic nature of the evolution of the sociuses, or the cohesive, multifaceted interconnected worldview of cultural markers, flows of capital, and flows of in/organic bodies from place to place, job to job, and feeling to feeling. O'Sullivan (2010) provides a reading and explanation of what Guattari's processual assemblage is, and what it means in terms of where we are now. The processual assemblage, as Guattari and O'Sullivan both emphasize, is the hopeful postcapitalist not-quite-Utopia that would represent a clean break with capital and capital generation being part and parcel of what determines who has the most sway in society. But within talking about this potential categorically radical shift in global culture and commerce, we have to be aware of how in/organic bodies function and create daisy chaining sets of differing, granular sets of rules, expectations, and ways of being that may blur the line between "globally culturally acceptable" and "true to self/others." Ultimately, to usher in the processual assemblage and start making room for a new societal expectation of cooperation over commerce, we have to be wary of the ways and means that the current regime of capitalism is actively perverting formerly radical ways of being that were meant to sabotage and usurp capitalism into softened cultural markers that, while they might maintain some of the original point of the movement, are ultimately just points of monetization. In doing this, we end up having to contend with the utopics inherent in Guattari's idealized global order, and what this means if we invoke the same terminology as possibly *new* ways and means of meaning-making. Meaning, we have to contend with the unfortunate fact of the matter that formerly radical acts of self-preservation and self-efficacy failed. And if we follow Guattari's line of thinking, we have to be careful with what terminology we repurpose and how we repurpose it, lest we repeat the same mistakes. We also have to understand how assembly (manifested through Butler [2015] and Hardt and Negri [2019]), closeness, and collocation can be reformatted to understand our entanglements with other bodies in processual assemblages. However, once we get to a better understanding of the possible degrees of entanglement present in Guattari's line of thinking and becoming, and the ways in which we can reconfigure our own collocation with activities that could help usher in the these changes, we all of a sudden open ourselves up to what Grosz (2018) refers to as ontoethical action, and what I end up terming ontoethical praxis.

In my fifth chapter, I close out this work by providing a retrofitted definition of what Grosz's ontoethics is and how we can begin to pick her tools up and use them in our own scholarly activist activities. Using ontoethics, we can start to look at glimmers of hope that have existed in videogame production and somehow outside of the grasp of the capitalist socius, and what those glimmers of hope might mean for a more comprehensive approach to "solving" some of the problems inherent to game production. I provide a list of five main issues that are the result of the diligence undertaken in this text in addition to ethnographic work done, what the daisy chaining implications of those problems are, and an ontoethical praxis that could be undertaken to start fixing these issues. I go further into depth to discuss the collocative elements present in unions and crunch that are not clearly examinable.

In the conclusive element, I go over a few issues that don't fit as cleanly into the theory-base that I have built but are still integral to understand in context and collocation *with* those theory elements. The first is a more industry-focused, example-led dive into unions and collective action: specifically, the part of immaterial labor forcing us to reconfigure how we think about unions. The second is the role of diversity, "initiatives," and gender renegotiation within current videogame production. By ending with these issues, I hope to be able to foreground how and where we might see progress being made in current videogame production, and where we need to go next.

NOTES

1. For a substantial discussion on what crunch is in a general sense, how it operates, and the devious ways that crunch is enacted and perpetuated in videogame production, see: "You Can Sleep Here All Night" by Ian Williams (2013), "The Recruitment of Passion and Community in the Service of Capital" by Aphra Kerr and John Kelleher (2015), and "The Perils of Book-Based Work" by Amanda Pettica-Harris, Johanna Weststar, and Steve McKenna. Each of these pieces discusses and defines crunch as "overwork" with extra situational and labor-related trappings.

2. PAX, E3, Gamescon, BlizzCon, CES, GDC, and DreamHack are prominent gaming conventions that take place in the US and abroad. Each of these conventions caters to a specific gaming niche. For example, BlizzCon is put on by game developer Blizzard, and is an annual showcase of upcoming content for their games.

Chapter 1

Multifaceted Manifestations

This book is one where positioning and embodied experiences are more important, and a more desirable end goal, than explanations of motivation regarding a broad swatch of people. In this chapter, I will give a broad stroke and theory-based understanding of what precarity is and what its discreet parts are made of according to various literature. Lauren Berlant's conception of cruel optimism is an important starting place to talk about the theorization of precarity. Cruel optimism presents a nuanced way of understanding the motivations at work in embodied experiences with videogame production that can facilitate precarity. Berlant, in *Cruel Optimism* (2012), defines cruel optimism as

> [relations . . . that exist] when something you desire is actually an obstacle to your flourishing. It might involve food, or a kind of love; it might be a fantasy of the good life, or a political book. [. . .] These kinds of optimistic relations are not inherently cruel. They become cruel only when the object that draws your attachment actively impedes the aim that brought you to it initially. (1)

To properly understand the initial allure of, and then the reticence and difficulty (both logistically and emotionally) of leaving, videogame production we must take into account the stickiness of affect, or emotionality, and how that stickiness exacerbates issues of attachment that have long been part and parcel of the productive element of videogame production. Once Berlant's theoretical contributions are established, I can examine the necessary discrete parts of cruel optimism that allow for the theorization of videogame production as an engine of subjectivation. Subjectivation in this book is understood to be a series of events, actions, cultural expectations, labor relations, affective and emotion entrapments and attachments that contribute to and shape a person's current present. In *History of Sexuality* (1988), Michel Foucault talks about subjectivity and subjectivation as historically constituted and situated "events," but not as "substances," meaning that, as a person experiences life, they are shaped by those experiences. Finally, I will examine how passion, precarity, and immaterial labor operate in relation to videogame production.

The most important theoretical concept that this book leverages comes from Lauren Berlant's book *Cruel Optimism*. By understanding and updating Berlant's conception of how cruel optimism happens and who it happens to, it is possible to understand how cruel optimism manifests in videogame production. It is important to understand cruel optimism as Berlant presents the concept. From her original definition, it will become easier to understand how cruel optimism functions in the specific material-discursive circumstances of videogame production. Cruel optimism in videogame production functions akin to a recipe. It needs certain ingredients to allow it to function. The concepts of precarity, passion, and immaterial labor describe material-discursive circumstances in which cruel optimism can exist and proliferate.

The first ingredient of cruel optimism is the setting. Where, exactly, can cruel optimism manifest? What are the conditions that it thrives in? By drawing on Lazzarato's definitional work of what immaterial labor is, the bounds and contours of immaterial labor become apparent. Within immaterial labor, affect and affective attachment become powerful subjectivating tools. Immaterial labor's goal is to produce surplus values of knowledge capital by subjectivating workers to accept heterogeneous working spaces that cater to certain types of people over others and value iterative, safe change over sweeping change. Immaterial labor enables institutional circuits that trap threats to production and allow for those problems to be isolated, which allows for production pipelines to minimally change or be interrupted. Cruel optimism exists here to allow workers to be subjectivated into conforming to institutional discourses that dictate what a productive body is versus a nonproductive body.

The second ingredient of cruel optimism is passion. In videogame production specifically, passion is operationalized as both a recruitment and a retention tool. Drawing from management studies, organizational psychology, entrepreneurial studies, and business studies, it will be possible to tease out a cohesive composite image of what "passion" can be defined as and then thought about in regard to videogame production. What about videogame production inspires passion? How has videogame production operationalized passion into a subjectivation tool? How does this operationalization create precarity? Videogame production is careful to show the playfulness of videogame production as a job and are careful to appeal to the aspect of workers "doing what they love." Passion is showcased and operationalized as a cultural fit tool, a meritocractic advancement component, and, ultimately, a way of subjectivating workers to accept that overwork, or crunch, is just a part of producing a truly sublime product: a case of "bleed for what you love." Cruel optimism rides on the coattails of that sentiment, driving workers to work harder, longer, and quicker in the hopes of recognition and meritocratic advancement.

The final ingredient of cruel optimism is precarity. How does overwork, casualization of work, job scarcity and insecurity, and outsourcing, contribute to precarity as it pertains to videogame production? In videogame production, precarity depends upon the next two ingredients of cruel optimism: passion and immaterial labor. When those two are established, precarity can exist as the sort of icing on the cake; the glue that keeps cruel optimism together in videogame production. Though "precarity" can pejoratively refer to how an industry is positioned (e.g., the precarity of the banking industry, housing bubbles, etc.), precarity needs support to exist. Precarity requires the conditionality of immaterial labor enabling work that is knowledge capital-generating, does not require prolonged physical presence, and is interconnected. Immaterial work can be sent elsewhere in the world should the price of keeping that labor in the US be too much. Once the conditionality is established, and there's an ever-present "threat" of losing the immaterial labor a body is responsible for (in this case outsourcing), passion can be operationalized and called upon to convince a worker to work harder, longer, and quicker. All in the name of producing a product in the medium that the person is "passionate" about.

By establishing these concepts as the "ingredients" of cruel optimism, it is possible to, finally, examine possible next steps in regard to precarity in videogame production. Are unions a ready-made answer? Does the model of a "union" that is largely predicated on and made for material labor provide an able method for workers to collectively bargain? The answers, unfortunately, become more muddy the further into the issue one looks.

CRUEL OPTIMISTIC ATTACHMENT

There is a necessary component of fantasy attached to cruel optimism: "the *affective structure* of an optimistic attachment involves a sustaining inclination to return to the scene of fantasy that enables you to expect that *this* time, nearness to *this* thing will help you or a world to become different in just the right way" (2). Fantasy allows for imaging new normals; situations beyond what is already not working. Berlant locates the willingness to engage with fantasy as an important aspect of cruel optimism, characterizing fantasy as "the means by which people hoard idealizing theories and tableaux about how they and the world 'add up to something'" (2). The search for normalcy and habitude are endemic to fantasy, and are bolstered by allowing affective attachments to anchor themselves *in* those fantasies. The characterization of affect and its implication in the act of attaching a person to a fantasy in such a way that that attachment, and the action of seeking being closer to that attachment, becomes damaging is important. Lisa Blackman and Couze Venn in "Affect" partially characterize "affect" as "nonverbal, nonconscious dimensions of experience [as] reengagement with sensation, memory, perception, attention and listening" (8). This becomes important when thinking through how attachments can be bolstered in fantasy. Affective investment in a desired object or a routine or thing is not always done consciously, or rather, with consciousness towards the decision of becoming "attached." Instead, affect greases the gears of attachment, creating a decision-making process that goes beyond a simple yes/no of whether to continue pursuing that thing. Affect creates emotional anchors to and around an object that change the simple yes/no decision-making process to "yes, but" and "no, but." Berlant characterizes affect as a way of finding habitude and normalcy (57), but also as an "[attachment] to the soft hierarchies of inequality [that] provide a sense of *their place in the world*" (194). It becomes a series of processes, of cognitions, actions, attachments, entrapments, feelings, labors, that produce the material-discursive positioning of a person within a suspended, temporal moment. The affective structure of cruel optimism is both the containing force of cruel optimism and one of its drivers. The return to fantasy that Berlant mentions is an iterative process. The iterative process can be as simple as rethinking a relationship, trying to make it work; downplaying perceived negative behaviors and highlighting perceived positive behaviors to paint an attainable picture of a happy life together. Or making a pros and cons list regarding a decision where objectivity is really relative, and the weights of both pros and cons can vastly differ because the allure of what is on the other side of that decision is greater than the desire to remain in the present situated experience.

Berlant makes a point again and again of saying that, regardless of how cruel optimism operates in any given situation, there is no shame to be had in it. Cruel optimism, she argues, isn't about doing the irrational just for the sake of irrationality—at the end of the day, it is about searching for normalcy and every-day-ness (54) in addition to establishing habitude (57). But what Berlant is building to is the *context* in which the processes of seeking normalcy and habitude occur. Berlant uses Bordowitz's 2001 film *Habit* to understand how habitude and searching for normalcy in late-stage capitalism exist in a constant temporal space of crisis. *Habit* mirrors Bordowitz's own attempt at creating an understanding of his historical present: how does his cruel optimism towards normalcy and habitude operate in a time frame and a body frame that is actively non-normal? Due to stacked cultural stigmas (queer identification and being HIV-positive), the temporality and feasibility of normalcy becomes a quest for the impossible due to unaccountable circumstances. The attachment towards, and the processual movement toward, a habitude of perceived normalcy while existing in a state of non-normalcy creates a discord that is impossible to soothe.

Berlant makes the point of saying that cruel optimism is about attachment to an object of desire (24). Objects of desire are "a cluster of promises [which] allow us to encounter what's incoherent or enigmatic in our attachments, not as confirmation of our irrationality but as an explanation of our sense of *our endurance in the object*, insofar as proximity to the object means proximity to the cluster of things that the object promises" (24). When I talk about cruel optimism in this book, I am talking about a two-fold thing: the first is the attachment of a body to an object of desire. In the case of videogame production, I hypothesize some possible object(s) of attachment as being cultural capital, "living a dream," and clout. As some of my informants in later chapters talk about, the idea of "living the dream" of being in videogames and having access to the cultural capital associated with a "cool" job becomes enticing enough to buy fully into a fantasy that videogame production perpetuates. Work while you play, play games for a living, passion: all characterizations of the clout associated with working in games. The second is that the object itself is not the "cruel" part. What makes videogame production and attachment to it "cruel" is the operationalization of passion to subjectivate workers into accepting the abuses of the industry in order to succeed. The operationalization of passion can manifest in several ways. For my informants, which I will talk more about in chapter 3, their passion for playing videogames, being part of a counterculture, or seeking and finding validation within videogames was a catalyst for wanting to pursue videogame production. The end result for my informants was almost word-for-word that they wanted to have a hand in creating something that people would play and enjoy.

In videogame production, the promises attached to the object of attachment are threefold. First, displaying how passionate a worker is presents a path to become the next well-known face of a videogame, like Todd Howard: meritocracy will recognize workers' commitment and reward them accordingly. Second is that the abuses that videogame production entail are defensible because that's just the culture of the job. Activities such as hazing or "passion-checking" are simply a cultural expectation of this type of job and a necessity to become successful. Third, having access to the cultural cache of "doing-what-you-love" marks a person as inherently "lucky"; that person does not have to work a job they hate, and in the case of videogame production, that person has the option to "play while they work," means that workers are seen as Miya Tokumitsu in *Do What You Love: And Other Lies about Success & Happiness* talks about the culture of "doing what you love" as one that you must suffer for, but one that is, ultimately, more fulfilling (49). Rationally, a person can look at these promises and see the vague nature and possible dangers. There are no concrete steps attached to these promises that produce verifiable results. Instead, popular media presents videogame production through interviews with well-known workers as less of a toxic subjectiation process and more of a challenge: a game to be won, and a proving ground for why that winner shouldn't be someone else. Everyone knows that "grinding" in videogames makes you stronger and makes it easier to progress. Yet, videogame production relies on these promises as a way of coaxing out the passion of potential workers.

It is important to remember that passion isn't a static interaction in an affective environment. Instead, it is just another process that is operating within, alongside, and in opposition to other processes. Those processes combine to form the affective moment that a person inhabits. Berlant says that "The set of dissolving assurances also includes meritocracy, the sense that liberal-capitalist society will reliably provide opportunities for individuals to carve out relations of reciprocity that seem fair and that foster life as a book of adding up to something and constructing cushions for enjoyment" (3). Cruel optimism thrives on the promise of a "good life," or some sort of equilibrium where precarity does not exist or is not actively fraying away: "upward mobility, job security, political and social equality, and lively durable intimacy" (3). All my informants for this book stated that they followed the career path that they did due to the promise of something better; something that they could either leave their mark on, or something that they could be a cultural affector for. Each person pursued videogame production to obtain something that they dreamed of having: stability for some, a home for others, enough capital to live comfortably for themselves, cultural cache and name recognition for others. They saw the videogame production industry as a thriving, vibrant entity that could accommodate their wishes for something better while also being able to see their passion bloom into physical things that people would interact with and absorb into their own affective processing.

The construction of the "the good life" encompasses the passion, the objects of attachment, the unsustainable promises, the endurance of people towards a goal, and the actual conceptual identity that this book is ascribing to videogame production. In short, the idea of "the good life" as a carrot dangling on a stick that people struggle toward is the containing unit of cruel optimism. Meritocracy and the neoliberal push for everyone and everything to be self-starting, autonomous, and professional but also wholly beholden to the whims of late-stage capitalism ultimately yield a decaying fantasy where hard work and gumption are still the capital of upward mobility. These beliefs are integral for the current survival and capitulation of the insidious ways and means by which videogame production imbricates passionate workers. If capital and cultural capital are the ultimate productive goal of late-stage capitalism, the core of it falls apart without productive, subjectivatable people.

Most specifically when people that believe they have an imperative function in what Aleena Chia (2019) calls a "new economy" are extricated (773). In *Disruptive Fixation* Sims (2018) talks about the early New School in NYC as an example of rampant subjectivation in this vein. Students from economically disadvantaged areas were brought into a highly technologized space and taught technological competencies and learning skills that would enable them to switch from knowledge-production job to knowledge-production job.

New methods of production that don't favor late-stage capitalism's model of producing surpluses of knowledge and cultural capital by way of breaking people into subjectivated production machines cannot occur on a large scale. Late-stage capitalism is concerned with producing as much capital as it can with as few noncontrollable parts as it can. This is where subjectivation, or cultural and material-discursive expectations of "work," become important. Late-stage capitalism subjectivates people to accept whatever conditions of work are most advantageous to production and not question those conditions. This subjectivation isn't always necessarily horrific, especially in immaterial labor in the West. Rarely is it a sweatshop narrative where workers are forced to work exceedingly long hours constantly in unsafe conditions for fractions of the wealth they are producing. Subjectivation can be as simple as subtle pressures to work overtime instead of relaxing, or just expecting that certain time periods of the year will require more work hours than other times. Subjectivation and cruel optimism work together to become part and parcel of what keeps workers actively engaged and *overworking* towards a goal or attachment. People are subjectivated to continue capitulating the idea that only hyperproductive bodies are of any use in this current productive era. However, there are cultural strata being gestured to as consolation prizes for workers to soften the fatalistic nature of this subjectivation. Working hard can earn more money, more cultural cache, more respect from bosses, more admiration from your peers. The only barrier to those things is working harder. Pockets of resistance occur, but the capitalist socius, which Deleuze and Guattari refer to in *Anti-Oedipus* as the "body" or form of capitalism which includes labor processes, social influence, and subjectivation, actively finds ways of consuming those pockets and monetizing them. Ultimately, this renders these sites of resistance as little more than overly idealistic pits of good intention that lead further into the hellscape of late-stage capitalism. For instance, something as simple as "being nice" has become a tool of capitalism. Tom Whyman, in his online article "What Is Cupcake Fascism" articulates that neoliberalism and late-stage capitalism have started to rely not on oppressive, autocratic structures to beat the populace into submission, but instead on militant *niceness* to bury any unseemly negativity that could lead to revolution: "Cupcake fascism asserts itself violently through something the infantilized subject holds deeply as an ideal. This ideal is *niceness*.

On the one hand, niceness is just what the infantilized subject thinks is lacking from the world [they are] hiding from." The example that Whyman uses to talk this concept through is 2011 postriots London. After tensions mounted over possible financial crisis and riots broke out, a piece of WWII propaganda reemerged. Keep Calm and Carry On (KCCO) found its way back into cultural relevance. Only, instead of KCCO in the face of bombing runs, the people of London were KCCO cleaning up after the riots. Instead of confronting the issues that caused the riots in the first place, and directing action towards social change in that regard, social media and news outlets infantilized the riots as "temper tantrums" and valorized those cleaning up as cooler heads prevailing. It is this pathological *need* for niceness to bury the ugliness in the world that allows for the capitalist socius to continue consuming and monetizing potentially revolutionary acts of resistance.

PASSION AND PRECARITY IN VIDEOGAME PRODUCTION

In the case of videogame production, passion is used as a recruiting, retention, and subjectivation tool. Workplace culture in videogame production is often created around the passion for playing videogames. In "Inside the Culture of Sexism at Riot Games," D'Anastasio outlines how the workplace culture and the workplace "fit" at Riot Games insists upon potential employees being "hardcore gamers." One informant that shared her story with D'Anastasio talked about the hiring process as being a constant push from the male hiring committee to see how passionate she was about playing videogames and to try and catch her lying about her passion. When the topic of raiding in *World of Warcraft* came up, the informant listed her raiding experience as above-average, and named some of the raids that she had cleared, and the hiring committee grilled her to see if she was lying because they couldn't seem to grasp that a woman could achieve those types of successes.

Kerr and Kelleher outline how, in community-management positions, passion is a buzzword that is used in job material to mask a grueling on-call schedule, few holidays off, and poor compensation. Kerr and Kelleher also note that "Passion was most frequently co-located with gaming knowledge and arguably, what many of these advertisements were doing was hailing fans and game players. This also, we suggest, excludes those who do not see themselves as passionate game players and blurs the boundaries between work and play" (185). As is the case with D'Anastasio's informant's experiences, passion is, again, being used as a metric to gauge culture fit and willingness to sacrifice to work in videogames. The way in which passion is collocated with knowledge of gaming in general, or with the particular game that is being recruited for, hints at the necessity of recruiting passionate workers to do the grueling labor that keeps games profitable as a service model. Without people that are amenable to that kind of labor, and subjectivated to be willing to endure overwork and the potential of that overwork not leading to the promise of stability and glamour that was promised, the model of making game content as a service to fans would fall apart.

In "The Perils of Book-Based Work," Pettica-Harris, Weststar, and McKenna look at how passion explicitly creates environments that are inherently anti-unionization. Their work looks at how passion is mobilized to first hook in talent by promising that workers will be working in "cool" environments (for instance, pizza and donut Fridays) (580), and then to systematically keep them hooked through stock options and kickbacks from sales that will trickle in over the span of years. Additionally, the way that blame is shifted away from human actors and onto the book is another insidious methodology of control. It's easy to be mad at a person for demanding that a worker work late or work unfair hours. It is much harder to be mad at a book; especially when the book, ostensibly, is the thing that recruited workers and mobilized workers in the first place to join the company. Pettica-Harris, Weststar, and McKenna say that the allure of "cool" food and a "cool" working environment for employees is a way of making it seem like the company cares about them while skirting the responsibility for their deteriorating health from eating junk food constantly, working under extreme pressure, and not taking care of their bodies (581). Pettica-Harris, Weststar, and McKenna set up the conditions where passion is, instead of just a mobilizing force now, a force of spite. The act of "production" invites workers to think of these jobs in videogame production as "cool" and "hip" instead of as precarious and awful. By appealing to the cultural capital of "working in videogames" and "being a cool job," these jobs carry certain expectations, like being ok with working 60, 70, 80 hour weeks (again, see: Mike Capps" 2008 IDGA comments[1]). The entire attitude of crunch and of old-style work-until-you-drop can be summed up with the saying "work hard, play hard." By having access to the cultural capital that few have (e.g., working in videogames), workers are expected to constantly prove that they belong there (Kunzelman, 2017).

Robin Johnson, in "Hiding in Plain Sight: Reproducing Masculine Culture at a Video Game Studio," outlines how hegemonic masculinity in production workplaces can be linked with "winning" or "putting in the effort to get better" at games (582). People who "win" more, or show more passion for getting better tend to be considered more masculine. Passion then becomes a workplace culture fit policing measure where those who lose or do show passion for winning become less masculine, and the passion that these workers *do* exhibit is discounted because it is not operationalized for production.

Workers who do not or cannot work crunch are considered less fit to work in the industry and share in the cultural cache. Bulut in "Playboring in the Tester Pit" talks about how the cultural cache of working within videogames is so appealing to some workers that they are willing to take pay cuts, work in abusive work environments, and contend with poor working conditions just to say that they work in videogames (243).

Another aspect of precarity that videogame production encourages is job insecurity. Contract labor and outsourcing create new contours to explore when talking about hiring practices, retention and advertising, and following passion into videogame production. Contract labor and outsourcing feed into cruel optimism by allowing management to operationalize the passion of workers to convince them to work harder, longer, and faster for the *chance* of upward mobility, which is more often than not an untruth. Contract labor and outsourcing also produce new contours when considering skill mastery. Just as material skills such as masonry require specialized physical skills and workplaces, videogame production, and software production in general, have their own specialized skills. Software knowledge, coding languages, process knowledge, or infrastructure knowledge are more valuable to capitalism than material knowledge since those knowledge sets are integral to producing knowledge and cultural capital. But with those competencies, new forms of precarity must be accounted for. No longer is software and immaterial knowledge production tools a privileged Western knowledge. Eastern European countries like Ukraine, Belarus, and Turkey, and third-world countries such as India, Malaysia, Iraq, and Iran are developing highly technologized sectors that are capable of doing the same work as Westerners at a fraction of the price. The faux-promise of possibly being hired full time, and the threat of losing contract work to outsourcing create another dimension of precarity within videogame production.

Software production as a field utilizes contract labor and what Spinuzzi, in *All Edge*, refers to as "swarming" (73) to accomplish tasks quickly, and then dissipate. A core team may work on the planning stages and preproduction of a software, then contract labor is brought in to help build prototypes and iterations of the software, and when that prototype is at a marketable stage, the labor force is disbanded back down to a core team. When that software needs to be tested, or other features added, contract labor can be brought back in to "swarm" those jobs, and then disbanded again. In a 2014 expose, Jason Schrier talked to Holden Link, publisher of GamesJobWatch, who said:

"It's weirdly common to hear about people getting laid off from the same company more than once—i.e., they get laid off, rehired, and laid off again in a span of two or three years, often without a different job in between," said Link. "Those scenarios are a vivid illustration of these kind of layoffs—the company didn't need someone for a few months, then decided they needed them full-time again until something else went wrong."

In videogame production, especially, contract labor is often brought on with the promised possibility of being made core members of a team once their contract is up. Rarely does this happen.

As outlined in a 2016 exposé called "The Game Industry's Disposable Workers," Colin Campbell details how contract labor in videogame production are constantly baited with the possibility of being brought on full time while still struggling with the reality of being contract labor. Campbell's informants reported that "they feel mistreated and even mislead by managers who dangle the possibility of full employment, but rarely follow through. In employment law circles, this is known as 'employment misclassification.'" One informant of Campbell's said: "[Game companies] put you on a year's contract and they say that it might end with a full-time position. You're in suspense until two weeks before your contract is up and then say 'oh we can't convert you.'" As production costs rise, videogame production is turning more and more to contract labor to even out the pay gap. Campbell speaks to Nate Gibson, an expert on employee misclassification, who says that hiring contract labor versus hiring full-time labor saves approximately 30% in costs for *each contractor hired in place of a full-time staff member*. In addition to the ability for an employer to simply fire contract labor when they are no longer needed, contract laborers do not receive insurance through the company contracting them, nor do they receive sick days, vacation days, or personal days. They are generally paid by the hour or by the day, which creates an environment for contract labor where time literally is money. Contract laborers in videogame production are often faced with work stipulations that were never made clear to them. Similarly, Campbell talks about one of their informants who worked as a video editor for a large publisher. He was informed, after he was hired, that he was employed by a contract firm and not the company itself. In addition to this omission, his work responsibilities and working hours shifted several times without his consent, while his wage stayed the same: "We never signed anything agreeing to [these changes], nor were we told it was happening," he says. "When one of my [contract] coworkers asked if it was negotiable, he was told no and that he could always look for another placement if he wasn't happy."

The factor that makes contract labor possible, which then makes job insecurity possible, is the practice of outsourcing, and the constant threat *of* outsourcing. In addition to the devastatingly stressful environments that videogame production takes place in, a good portion of that work is outsourced, contributing to further job instability and precarity. In "OUTSOURCING: Video Game Art Is Increasingly 'To Go,'" Paul Hyman examines how the outsourcing practices of videogame art was an early harbinger of things to come. The company he profiles, THQ (today known as THQNordic), is a multibillion dollar triple-A videogame producer that refers to outsourcing as "distributed development." Hyman references THQ having outsourced 20–25% of their art asset development in 2008, whereas today they outsource somewhere around 80% of their art asset development. Their in-house production is now primarily game systems, proprietary art assets, and marketing/branding. THQ's rampant outsourcing speaks to the nature videogame production process: what you keep in-house will end up costing you more than outsourcing. The majority of the art assets that THQ's internal developers outsource are to developing countries with burgeoning tech sectors like India; this means that, for what would cost these internal developers millions of dollars to develop in-house, they can outsource for it to be developed for a fraction of that price. In "'EA Spouse' and the Crisis of Video Game Labor," Dyer-Witheford and de Peuter talk about what was then a rising concern, saying "there is an intensifying trend toward outsourcing game development work, with big studios such as EA on a global quest, from Shanghai to Ho Chi Minh, for new sources of skilled game labor. Within even its most privileged echelons, there are no certainties under conditions of globalization" (602). According to Chebotareva in "Why Ukrainian CG Market is One of the Driving Forces Behind the Success of the Games Industry," burgeoning third-world tech sectors still see a massive share of outsourcing, but new tech sectors such as Eastern Europe are presenting a more enticing alternative due to "cultural concerns" and language barriers.

Cruel optimism is enabled through precarity. If there is the promise of a "better life," or advancement, workers would be foolish to not work to their full potential to achieve more, right? It is exactly this mindset that allows for institutions to keep moving the goal posts as capital generation dictates the need to move them. American neoliberalism, according to Julie Wilson, boils down to humans not being encouraged "to understand, much less critique or try to change, their society. Rather, they should be trained for competition in the market. For only via competition can individuals realize their freedom, which, for neoliberals, means realizing their place and purpose in the unfolding of spontaneous market order" (63). By encouraging unchecked competition among people in a continually globalized market, precarity becomes a control mechanism insofar as the threat of losing a job, it being outsourced, and a body being rendered redundant are used to keep workers working at their limits and being *accepting* of that. But what force can be tapped to make people do this?

Whose Passion, and Why Does It Matter?

In game studies, and even digital media studies, the concept of "passion" is not well-understood in regard to how it is leveraged to gauge work, success, enjoyment of a job, or as a catalyst to inspire workers (or customers) to take greater pride in their "brand." It is important, then, to turn to a corpus where passion *is* well-theorized and documented to help us assemble our own working definition. In management studies, organizational psychology, entrepreneurial studies, and business studies, passion is leveraged as means of understanding intention behind a set of actions, a person's drive to succeed at something, or a person's willingness to persevere in precarious circumstances to achieve a goal. Passion, as defined by Murnieks, Mosakowski, and Cardon in "Pathways of Passion," is a strong inclination towards certain activities over others that acts as an agent of influence regarding choices, relationship-building, or pursuance of certain paths of education or vocational training (1586). Baum and Locke, in "A Multidimensional Model of Venture Growth," characterize how entrepreneurial studies approach passion as growth vector due to the personal nature of both passion and entrepreneurship: without passion for one's business model, growth is difficult (292). Thorgren and Wincent, in "Passion and Challenging Goals" say that passion "is a strong inclination toward a self-defining activity that people like, find important and in which they invest time and energy" (2318). They hypothesize that, as an entrepreneur becomes more ensconced in a culture of self-starting and self-sustaining work habits, that they will exhibit more harmonious passion and obsessive passion as well. Harmonious passion refers to streamlining their business model, creating cohesive marketing and modeling, and creating more uniformity across platforms, while obsessive passion refers to doing the aforementioned during times usually designated for leisure or non-job activities. This means their drive for success, and the passion that they have towards the *idea itself* and ensuring its success, consumes more non-work and personal time than similar ideas/initiatives might for nonentrepreneurial workers. This speaks to enculturation as a powerful subjectivating measure in entrepreneurial circles: the more belief that one has in their idea, and the more time that one spends thinking about, workshopping, and obsessing about their idea, the more successful the idea should be. And inversely, if adequate passion is not invested in a book, then the chances are greater that the initiative will fail.

Another important concept within passion to understand is "grit." Duckworth, Peterson, Matthews, and Kelly, in "Grit: Perseverance and Passion for Long-Term Goals" define grit as a subset of passion; an augmentation to, and explanation of success within passion. They identify grit as an x-factor of sorts that determines why some people achieve more than peers of equal intelligence, privilege, and station. They define this concept as "perseverance and passion for long-term goals. Grit entails working strenuously toward challenges, maintaining effort and interest over years despite failure, adversity, and plateaus in progress" (1087–88). They define the ideal "gritty" body as being someone that approaches success in their venture as if they were running a marathon: perseverance and stamina are the keys to leveraging grit. Grit and passion create an entanglement that is difficult to undo; without one, the other is bound to fail according to them. Whereas the previous literature was concentrated in entrepreneurial endeavors, Duckwork, Peterson, Matthews, and Kelly identified the concept of grit as a measure of success across academia, medicine, journalism, law, banking, and painting (1089). The people that they interviewed talked at length about how and why they persevered through adversity and precarity, and the reason was that each body had some form of affective attachment to their area of expertise. Grit, for these people, exemplified a willingness to grind against precarity *because* of the passion that those people had for their expertise. For some, grit was augmented with a humanitarian or humanistic spin. Some informants were convinced that the world needed their passion and their passion-project to come to fruition because, without it, the world would be a less full place. For others, grit augmented a desire to achieve more: more than their peers, more than their parents, friends, etc. In both cases, grit presented an interesting and useful term for gauging how *personal* passion is meted out in any project. As with most entrepreneurial endeavors, grit is predicated on an ultimately neoliberal ideation that the project at hand, or the underlying passion, is *necessary* for enriching the world around the project-owner.

Eugenia Siapera, in the chapter "Affective Labor and Media Work" in *Making Media* (2019), collocates entrepreneurialism with the casualization of labor, and more insidiously, how entrepreneurial scholarship has helped to craft an Ideal Type (Weber, 1942) of person whose ethics, vision, and passion enable them to be successful. I talk more about Ideal Types in later chapters, but for our purposes here, "Ideal Types" can be considered situationally perfect bodies whose entire subjectivity falls within specific contours for specific argument examples that are often unattainable and without *real* real-world implication. Siapera draws a rather stark image of media workers who do not exhibit these entrepreneurial attributes. Without the strategic vision and the will to contort their in/organic bodies into shapes that match the outlines of media production popularized by people like Jarvis (2009) and Spinuzzi (2015), bodies do not have a future in journalism or media work. Siapera draws this dire picture based on how authors like Jarvis and Spinuzzi, alongside Baum and Locke, Thorgren and Wincent, and Duckworth et al., all predicate "success" on capitalistic standards by vouching for an almost Silicon Valley-esque model of a start-up: capitalize on a niche passion, build a community centered around that passion, short-sell the community. These types of passionate explosions not only create grounds for passion being a battery for content creation or, rather, for gauging how engaged and how much/how quickly a body can create content, but also as, quite literally, a battery to break down barriers between audience and creator, passion and monetizability, and affect and "content." Too, the aspect of short-selling a community comes in a variety of forms, but most all of them revolve around behavior or content choices that yield capital. A common example of short-selling that has become prevalent in content creation communities is taking platform deals that upend or destroy milieus communities create so that the creator can capitalize. This is most apparent in artists or podcasters signing to certain platforms, streamers abandoning platforms to take multi-year, big-payout contracts, and even videogame creators publishing through certain publishers or platforms that have predatory histories but promise more money upfront or on the gross.

Siapera in this chapter uses journalism to shine a light on how *affective* labor has become a necessary labor to undertake in order to be deemed successful; creating a bond with an audience, curating a certain emotional and affective response to the types of material that are covered, and even how the body in question portrays their affective inculcation with the subject matter. Most importantly, though, is the aspect of collocating passion *with* the audience, which in turn creates a milieu, or specific social space with distinct rules, affects, and expectations, that is specific to that group and *favors* that group's ontonological approach to the world around them and the content they are engaging with. Siapera (2019) says that this affective labor "can produce positive externalities, such as communities and social networks, which can on the one hand lead to alternative forms of production and life, but on the other hand can be appropriated and commodified by capital (287)." The process of commodification goes hand in hand with the spirit of entrepreneurialism that Siapera alludes to but never explicates; to garner success in today's media work sphere, capital (in this case knowledge capital) must be interwoven into passion. Additionally, the collocation of passion with the object of attachment is necessary to open new avenues of capital generation by which the spirit of entrepreneurialism becomes manifest. Create a community that amasses certain numbers of clicks/views/subscribers/etc. and suddenly businesses like PayPal Honey, MeUndies, NordVPN, Raid: Shadow Legends, and HelloFresh might be keen to partner with that creator—of course, the creator is responsible for making that sponsorship seem organic and like what they are doing is furthering their ability to reach out towards that object of attachment, but often the systems and expectations in place are opaque both from the creator and the companies, which leaves the community in the dark about the ulterior motives behind those types of partnerships.

The affective dimensions of the media work that Siapera is outlining obviously is quite central to the entrepreneurialism of certain online content creation communities such as YouTubers or Twitch streamers. Jamie Woodcock in "The Affective Labor and Performance of Live Streaming on Twitch (2020)" exemplifies what Siapera talks about in terms of creating communities of passion. Often, we see content creators, especially in videogamic sectors, engage with somewhat dubious practices such as taking gambling sponsorships when that content creator's audience is well under gambling age,[2] or content creators engaging with problematic communities. One example of that is popular YouTuber Tobuscus making content with murderer Kyle Rittenhouse and leaning into certain alt-right conspiracy mouth-piecing while also having a problematic past himself.[3] These types of turns in content creation or streaming style present interesting embodied examples of the pressure of entrepreneurialism and content creation. Not only as examples of passionate betrayal, but also as examples of passionate exploitation. Hardt and Negri (2000) talk about the commodification of emotion to an extent, and how flows of capital often negotiate new "acceptable" behaviors. Tobuscus and ItsSliker (and to a larger extent, Twitch's problematic relationship with gambling since at least late 2017) exemplify how capital (in terms of content creation, that equates to money, popularity/charting of content, and social mobility) can create agencements in the milieu of these communities which in turn might allow for creators to make choices like these and not immediately lose what they built. The key, though, is not the passion itself exhibited by community or creator; instead, passion is acting as an *excuse* for the behavior engaged in, thus creating another layer of abstraction between community—content creator—passion—and problematicity. But the baseline for how these types of situations can even come about comes back to cruel optimism: there is affective attachment to the object of fixation that is embedded in entrepreneurialism. Regardless of whether that is a game, *creating* games, creating content *about* games, creating content that, on a meta level, reviews games culture. All these types of labor might have separate ontologies and their own specific, embodied milieu, but the impetus for these examples boil down to the basest examples of affective attachment and the necessity to create lines of ingress towards being closer to those objects. And all of this falls neatly in line with the types of entrepreneurial scholarship examined above.

So in addition to an entrepreneurial spirit (Thorgren and Wincent, 2013) and in addition to grit (Duckworth et al., 2007), we now must contend with the aspect of affective attachment—another aspect of cruel optimism and another aspect of generalized precarity. Though similar to the types of passionate exploitation present in videogame production, this section's discussion about content creation and passion only exemplifies yet another facet of the linkage between labor, cruel optimism (*especially* the aspect of proximity and a body doing whatever is necessary to attain proximity to the object of attachment), and precarity. It also only acts as a very specific example of the ways in which passion and cruel optimism work. This discussion needs one further clarification, though: the type of labor that videogame production and content creation embody are fundamentally mental and emotional activities. They are not directly linkable to difficult, manual labor that does not require the types of affective malleability that content creation and videogame production necessitate. Similar to the types of labor that Siapera highlighted, and the types of labor that Hardt and Negri speak about. Emotional, creative, affectively driven types of labor that do not necessarily require the same in/organic bodily necessities are different and require a refined discussion around what the nonphysical might mean in terms of labor.

Immaterial Labor and Affect

To understand further how and why passion and precarity become intertwined in videogame production to create the material-discursive conditions that it currently subsists in, it is important to understand the *type* of labor being performed. Immaterial labor, as defined by Lazzarato is "the labor that produces the informational and cultural concept of the commodity" (134). Lazzarato builds from what Marx, in *Grundrisse* (1858), talks about regarding the dichotomy of labor when machines take over the strenuous, repetitive labor types that material labor subsists on. Marx says that workers

> [step] to the side of the production process instead of being its chief actor. In this transformation, it is neither the direct human labor, he himself performs, nor the time during which he works, but rather the appropriation of his own general productive power, his understanding of nature and his mastery over it by virtue of his presence as a social body—it is, in a word, the development of the social individual which appears as the great foundation-stone of production and of wealth. (705)

This means that, as machinic, inorganic labor sources are instituted to offload the strenuous, repetitive nature of material labor, the human inculcated in these types of labor becomes responsible for using and applying knowledge to supplement the rote labor, or what we can term "knowledge production." Instead of being concerned with creating a physical "thing" that has its own static capabilities, quirks, and positioning that requires physicality to change those aspects, immaterial labor is concerned with creating knowledge capital. Additionally, knowledge production relies much less on physical labor than material production does. Instead of performing types of labor such as heavy lifting, welding, or structural building, knowledge production relies on "light" physical labor through which knowledge capital is produced. Typing, drawing, clay rendering, walking, standing, and playing are examples of the type of physical labor needed to create knowledge capital. Knowledge production utilizes affective, mindful, and psychical energy in the same way that physical production utilizes physical, kinetic, and corporeal energy. The labor involved with making a videogame involves using immaterial knowledge-based skills to create sign-based systems and architecture that can be changed easily. Material labor is required for things like data entry, proto-typing, and interfacing with colleagues, but the bulk of the labor being done is nonmaterial. Immaterial labor in industries like videogame production does not produce a physical architecture that depends on utilizing physical labor with very little immaterial labor for it be functional or to be changed.

Hardt and Negri (2000) talk about immaterial labor in three broad categories: design and manufacturing, data procurement and architecture, and affective labor or "the creation and manipulation of affects" that create "products [which include] a feeling of ease, well-being, satisfaction, excitement, passion—even a sense of connectedness or community" (96). Videogame production lives in the third kind of immaterial labor that Hardt and Negri talk about: affective immaterial labor. Production itself is propped up on the creation of creative, affective experiences that instill in users some sort of emotional attachment or experience. Therefore, this presents us with a fundamentally different type of labor to negotiate the material-discursive circumstances of as well as a fundamentally different set of metrics through which to gauge "success." Immaterial labor functions to enable knowledge production by creating pathways of subjectivation in which precarity and passion combine to form cruel optimism. By enabling knowledge production as a new arena of production, neoliberalism allows for production to become a competition in which "winners" work more, produce more, and sacrifice more.

In videogame production, this overwork manifests as and is operationalized through "passion." Passion relies on, and is invigorated by, a person's willingness to persevere in precarious circumstances to achieve a goal and drive for success. Passion is, then, used to subjectivate workers into always working harder, longer, and quicker not only as a meritocratic dimension but also a precarious dimension. This type of overwork harkens back to the discussion about entrepreneurialism insofar as the same metrics of success are shared: the more passion that is plied into a product, and the more affect that is imbued into an object, the more successful that project should be. However, meritocratic advancement in videogame production often does not account for passion because of how nebulous and unaccountable the concept of operationalizing passion is! That, taken with the fact that passion means vastly different things for different bodies in videogame production creates much the same situation with granularity that the word "precarity" renders.

There are multifaceted manifestations within each that create new agencements, new ontologies, and new contours that are unaccountable within capital generation. However, there is enough of a shared understanding of the productive power of affect and emotionality in *maintaining* collocation to an object of attachment that the word passion can be freely thrown around in parlance to mean anything from Mike Epps' infamous admonition that, if workers are not prepared to work at least 60 hour weeks and expect extended periods of crunch, that they do not belong in videogame production, all the way to the "story" of Todd Howard that is rolled out every award show that makes it seem like his journey was not one of egregious nepotism, but one or pure passion and hard work when we know that this is not the case.

Capital-generation in videogame production dictates that, if a worker is not doing "enough" (however *that* is defined, which is beyond the scope of this book), that work can be outsourced to developing countries, or a new, younger body can be brought in to do the same job for less pay simply because of the cultural cache of working in videogames in North America. All of this taken together forms what cruel optimism looks like in videogame production in North America from a top-down, generalist viewpoint. The type of labor expected has multiplicative, opaque requirements that vary from project to project, studio to studio, even worker to worker. This is where a generalized understanding of precarity becomes applicable to this type of labor. "Precarity" as an umbrella term is useful to do a lot of heavy theoretical lifting that does not directly point to specific characteristics of, instances of, or entanglements with the underlying elements of precarity. However, this book's entanglement with cruel optimism and the capitalist socius' need for subjectivatable bodies begs for closer inspection of precarity. I do not believe that precarity is a static thing, nor is it singular in nature. On its own, it can function as a way of talking about a situation or person, but it can also accompany and compliment the types of labor being performed in videogame production. Precarity can be a paired attribution to a person who is experiencing some negative circumstance, or even *sets* of circumstances. Precarity shifts and changes to suit circumstances and labor conditions. It morphs to encompass and exacerbate personal attachments to objects, people, or concepts. It spills out from singular events, encompasses fallout and preceding circumstances of events. In my third chapter, I will move towards a multiplicative theorization of precarit*ies* as a way to encompass these attributions.

WHAT NOW, WHAT NEXT?

This chapter has defined several concepts and made a case for a theoretical understanding of what precarity is, how it might manifest in certain circumstances, and under what conditions it might become exacerbated. Passion, as a concept, is a way of gauging a person's commitment to a thing over other things. Business and entrepreneurial studies consider passion as a driving metric in understanding success: the more of oneself that is committed to an idea or a book, the more success that that book will have. Immaterial labor, or "labor that produces the informational and culture concept of the commodity" (Lazzarato, 2014, 134), creates new forms of precarity that are not present in material labor. These precarities pose less of a bodily-injury risk, and are more focused on job insecurity in the forms of contract labor and outsourcing. Within videogame production, passion is leveraged as a way of justifying contract labor positions and job insecurity: those that are willing to show their passion in the form of labor will be rewarded with full-time positions, less precarious working conditions, and less job insecurity (Johnson 2013a). Passion is also used as a recruitment and retention tool within videogame production, and as a workplace policing measure. D'Anastasio's example of Riot's toxic recruiting culture, and how one informant reported being subjected to extensive questions about her *World of Warcraft* experience, are commonplace as far as passion being used as a workplace policing method. Within videogame production, passion is used to create environments that are inherently anti-union because of the valorization of overwork (Pettica-Harris, Weststar, McKenna, 580).

As previously stated, the goal of this book, and the intended academic contributions are not to make generalizable or anthropological characterizations of an entire group of people. I have used this chapter to lay out, theoretically, what precarity *should* or *could* be. There are forms of precarity in this chapter that can apply to certain circumstances or job-types that won't transfer to other circumstances or job-types. What this chapter theorizes is an impersonal understanding of "precarity" as an umbrella term. The literature I have reviewed in this chapter talks at length about characteristics and conditionalities of precarity, and is useful for establishing contexts to try and examine precarity in.

Cruel optimism presents a very convincing way of understanding motivation regarding peoples' choice to stay in videogame production or to pursue videogame production. The concept accounts for passion as both a driving force in subjectivation and as an overarching explanation of how videogame production can keep people hooked into potentially damaging or traumatic situations. It accounts for the necessity of seating this entire theoretical argument in immaterial labor. Without knowledge capital as the goal of the activity being discussed, passion and precarity assume different roles, answer to different material-discursive and ontological imperatives, and cannot be understood in the same ways. It also highlights how neoliberalism enables precarity by decentering agency from producers and instead focusing on productive capacity as the telling "worth" of a body.

What these theories fail to account for is the individual, embodied experiences of people working in videogame production. These theories lend themselves to making theoretical claims regarding how labor operates and how precarity manifests, but integrated world capitalism, the capitalist socius, and platformization do not take into account the people involved in these processes, nor the affective dimensions of what a body is processing through and experiencing. Cruel optimism, on the other hand, accounts for who, what, and why people that are involved in videogame production act, feel, and processes in the ways that they do. But what cruel optimism cannot account for is the embodied experience of the individuals involved in production. As Berlant reminds us when she is first sketching the contours of cruel optimism, this concept is an understanding of how capitalism and neoliberalism are privileging certain bodies and modes of consumption over others (3). The purpose of this book, and the purpose of Berlant's work, is not to make a sweeping generalization regarding intentionality. Berlant's work is more concerned with how the affective contours of bodily processing render themselves porous and nonsensical. What this book is interested in, on the other hand, is taking the singular, embodied experiences of people that are at work in various positions in videogame production and giving them a platform to share their truths. Cruel optimism can explain certain aspects of decision-making, especially how affect and emotionality play into decision-making regarding constructs of capital, but it cannot produce the personal truths of those that are involved in the industry for better or for worse. In the next chapter, I will go over my methodological approaches to this book in addition to my understanding of the impact those choices have on this book.

NOTES

1. In a panel at 2008's International Game Developers Association's (IDGA) annual conference, Mike Capps, head of Epic Games, stated in a panel that working 60 hours a week or more was standard practice at Epic and that those who are not willing to work those hours should seek employment elsewhere, or will be weeded out very quickly.

2. At the time of publishing, Twitch.TV recently came out to ban certain unlicensed types of gambling on their platform. See: Hern, 2022 for a more comprehensive understanding of how streamer ItsSliker scammed money off other streamers to gamble.

3. Tobuscus made a few videos with murderer Kyle Rittenhouse, and openly endorsed Rittenhouse's "game" seen in a clip by YouTube user trashpilepunk from

one of Tobuscus's 2022 streams. Additionally, Tobuscus has a history of accusations against him that involve raping a former partner, drug and alcohol abuse, and physical and mental abuse of former partners. See: Spangler (2016) for a more nuanced account.

Chapter 2

Systematics of Precarity

Or, How the Capitalist Socius Ascribes Value to Precarity

As I discussed in the previous chapter and in Roadmapping, the word precarity is used widely and, depending on the circumstances, positioning of literature, affects, temporalities, and a litany of other multiplicative, compounding identities, demarcations, and contours, mean wildly different things for similar people. Precarity, as a term, often acts as a catch-all for many different, nuanced situations that are granular in their precariousness, and to what level people may find that situation "precarious." The need for specificity when looking at and defining precarity is paramount to our ability as scholarly activists to figure out how to move past simply naming a situation as precarious, and start offering ways of *actioning* those situations.

Before we start, I want to discuss cruel optimism's role and some Deleuzoguattarian concepts' functionality in this chapter because these concepts build upon, intersect, and contour each other to provide the undergirding that is needed to prop up current videogame production. Meaning, each of the concepts this chapter examines is directly undergirded by or supported through cruel optimism. Cruel optimism in videogame production is too inextricably linked to the integrated systems of capital that keeps production running, and to the capitalist socius itself, to extract it from our conceptualization of precarity as a multiplicative set of operating circumstances.

The trappings of immaterial labor feed into job insecurity by way of casualization of labor. Casualization of labor allows for the operationalization of passion by way of using it as a metrics to judge worthiness or fit and also as a way of shifting blame from poor management structures (e.g., this game failed because you, individual worker, weren't passionate enough to put in the extra hours). Poor management structures allow for the projection of inflated timelines or workflows that become impossible to consistently stay in line with. Failure to stay in line with these structures leads to crunch. Crunch leads to passionate exploitation (again, if you aren't passionate enough about videogames to work this crunch for this project, you don't deserve to be here; there are plenty of more passionate people to replace you). Passionate exploitation lays quite snuggly in how the capitalist socius (Deleuze and Guattari, 1983) functions to consolidate floes of capital generation via overproduction. The capitalist socius's main goal is autopoiesis via production, and it relies on outside means to overload bodies with information, or overcoding, and to force those bodies into willingly perpetuating the cycle of production via subjectivation. In regard to videogame production in relation to the capitalist socius, the two are not competitors or separate entities. Instead, they are companions. The capitalist socius overloads bodies with cultural markers regarding videogames (they're fun, they're cool, when you make them all you do is play at work, etc.) to overcode workers into becoming objects of production that must adhere to the idea that videogames, and videogame production, have to be the way that they are, and must be guarded, lest their form of subjectivation that is allowing them to survive is threatened.

Cruel optimism's place in all of this is to act as lubricating fluid between steps. To navigate between these steps, there must be some *reason* to engage with them in the first place. One thing that is so enticing about using cruel optimism to contour the fluid mechanics of precarity is that it doesn't require coherence or the ability to pinpoint the *why* of why someone is attached to or enamored with something. Berlant, in *Cruel Optimism* (2012), says,

> To phrase "the object of desire" as a cluster of promises is to allow us to encounter what's incoherent or enigmatic in our attachments, not as confirmation of our irrationality but as an explanation of our sense of *our endurance in the object*, insofar as proximity to the object means proximity to the cluster of things that the object promise, some of which may be clear to us and good for us while others, not so much. (23–24)

The cluster or promises that ultimately seem to lure bodies into videogame production revolve around cultural clout (Bulut, 2015), the overlauded concept of suffering for one's art meeting the intersection of doing-what-you-love (Tokumitsu, 2014), and ultimately, parlaying one's passion for videogames (be it playing, watching, the culture, etc.) into ultimately creating something that may influence or spark the same passion in others, regardless of the self-imposed hardships. The cluster of promises borders on fetishizing the idea of creating games or being somehow involved and invested in that space. Berlant says, too, that

What's cruel about these attachments, and not merely inconvenient of tragic, is that the subjects who have x in their lives might not well endure the loss of their object/scene of desire, even though its presence threatens their well-being, because whatever the *content* of the attachment is, the continuity of its form provides something of the continuity of the subject's sense of what it means to keep on living on and to look forward to being in the world. (24)

The object of attachment is different for each person you talk to, of course, but there seems to be a consistent nexus point for most everyone I have spoken to where their embeddedness in videogames creates an inextricable part of their personhood that, without it, they wouldn't be who they want to be.

Cruel optimism also provides succinct, compelling ground for discussing what specific parts of the situations examined can act as the objects of attachment themselves. Without an object, set of actions, outcome, etc. to attach to and gesture towards, precarity becomes much less focused. But, it is important to remember that cruel optimism is not the end-all-be-all explanation for their manifestation, continuity, or parasitism. Again gesturing to intersectionality, a cruelly optimistic attachment forms one area of a much larger and much more complex composite picture.

Before I go any further with the harsh theory that I am going to engage with, I want to note some other theorists that, while helpful and potentially leagues more accessible than Deleuze and Guattari's unmediated work, do not quite provide the theoretical rigor or the access to conceptual building blocks that this project requires. Work like Dyer-Witheford and de Peuter's *Games of Empire* (2009) and Deuze's *Media Work* (2007) both pull from similar areas of theory that I engage with in this work, but they do so in abstracted ways. Meaning, they are engaging with these theories in spaces where in/organic actants are not necessarily the main consideration. Work like theirs, their component work, and the great swath of work that has spawned from them is incredibly important to media studies and game studies as a whole, and I am in debt to many of those pieces, they do not provide the theoretical rigor that I need in order to make clear the type of ontological turn necessary to affect the labor structure of videogame production. This is not a media studies-centric book, after all. Therefore, the theoretical requirements for this type of work are inherently different and require flexibility. Deleuze and Guattari, tempered with scholars like Grosz and O'Sullivan, create the perfect milieu through which exegeses around things like cultural capital, agencements around labor milieus, and understandings of bodies can emerge in new, challenging ways.

IS A CHECKLIST AN ASSEMBLAGE
OR AN AGENCEMENT?

I will provide a quick contextualization and explanation of a few key terms that I use in this section. According to Deleuze and Guattari (1983), the capitalist socius is a social "body," or an assembly of productive, social entities, that are responsible for production of resources. In the case of late-stage capitalism and videogame production, the resource being produced is monetizable units of cultural production. The videogame production industry is firmly ensconced in systems of capitalism: precarity in production labor that forces workers to work themselves well past exhaustion or face replacement (Bulut, 2014 and 2015; Kerr and Kelleher, 2015; Williams, 2013 and 2018; Weststar and Legault, 2017), outsourcing to third-world asset firms (Hyman, 2008), and the use of passion for videogames as an industry recruitment and retention tool and as a gate keeping mechanism for employee progress (Bulut, 2014 and 2015; Johnson, 2018; Deuze, Martin, and Allen, 2007; Kerr and Kelleher, 2015; Kuchlich, 2005; Sotaama, 2007; Parker, Whitson, and Simon, 2017). The work hours during production cycles are grueling (Johnston, 2013b; Dyer-Witheford and De Peuter, 2006; Bulut, 2014 and 2015; Llerena, Burger-Helmchen, Cohendet, 2009); the work environments reinforce negative binaries such as hypermasculinity and antifeminism (Johnston, 2013a; Fisher and Harvey, 2013; Hacker, 1979 and 1981; Salter and Blodgette, 2012), and human bodies are readily axiomatized as sources of capital (Gallagher et al., 2017; DiSalvo et al., 2007). This means that, as social and cultural issues reach a threshold of recognizability in society at large, the bodies in question in that movement become more easily subjectivizable and exploitable.

Assemblages and agencements are two terms that are heavily leveraged throughout this work and provide interesting ways of reimaging our imbrications with labor and passion. I am taking assemblages to refer to what Deleuze and Guattari spoke of in *A Thousand Plateaus* (1980) as constant becomings, comings-together, and reorigination of bodies in systems and hierarchies. Assemblages, roughly, gesture towards a chaotically systematized framework: in/organic bodies enter into union with other in/organic bodies, create concepts and conceptual frameworks, and initiate becomings by way of intensities and libidinal energies flowing in and through the assemblage. Becomings roughly equate to the psychical equivalent of potential energy; an object (or body) is acted upon, transferring energy into it which is then released when the object moves. Becomings function in a similar way, except instead of kinetic energy, becomings encompass a set of possible changes that are both effected by and directly effect affect, mental and psychical energy, *and* physical or proximal spatiotemporal changes. Libidinal energies, similar in metaphor to becomings, are the acute set of actions or circumstances that spur a body into a becoming. This energy can be sexual, per the name, affective, emotional, psychical, physical, sociocultural, or even random. Agencements are part of assemblages. Roughly, agencements translate to the material-discursive, theoretical, and embodied contoured edges of different becomings. Sort of like movable walls, except without the spatiotemporal lockedness of a wall. Like assemblages, agencements are always in the process of forming and reforming.

Something that will come up a bit in this chapter and again in chapter 4 is schizorevolution and ethicoaesthetics. Schizorevolution, as referenced in *Anti-Oedipus* (1983) refers to functionally "broken" ways of thinking, becoming, and perceiving the world around a body; ways that could, in fact, usher in new ways of meaning making. Deleuze and Guattari make liberal use of psychoanalytic concepts to refer to becomings, means, and concepts on the plane of immanence that actively seek to circumvent and subvert the capitalist socius. I fully acknowledge the problematicity of invoking the terminology "schizo-" when trying to reference systems of subjectivation and becoming that fundamentally break with institutionally acceptable rhetorics and semiotics. While potentially verdant ground at the time of writing *Anti-Oedipus* for thinking through ways of circumventing institutional semiotics, referencing mental illness in the ways that schizorevolution do make it difficult without some form of disclaimer to maintain theoretical rigor when thinking about how bodies of all flavors interact with videogame production. The term ethicoaesthetics come up with schizorevolution almost on a one-to-one basis in Guattari's work (especially in *Molecular Revolution* and *Three Ecologies*). Ethicoaesthetics are new ways of meaning making that attempt to circumvent objects of power and formal rule. Ethicoaesthetics usually refer to schizorevolutionary actions: actions taken in ways and means that fundamentally usurp subjectivation methodologies of the capitalist socius.

I am taking "hypermasculinity" to mean what Mosher and Sirkin (1988) identified as an attitude or state of mind that (a) exhibits a callous sexual attitude toward women, (b) believes that violence is manly, and (c) that experiencing danger is exciting. By using this definition, hypermasculinity in videogames doesn't just become a pejorative term to deride machismo, but instead becomes a checklist by which we can assess videogames, people, and workplace cultures.

By referring to "body," I am referring to multiple different understandings of what a body is/what constitutes a body: a human body, or a worker, or videogame production worker, refers to an organic human body and does not reference technical attachments or becomings unless otherwise noted (for this definition, I am mostly working off of Grosz's work around bodies [1994]). The capitalist socius (or capitalist body) refers to a social body defined by

Deleuze and Guattari (1983) that relies on outside means to overload bodies with information, or overcode, and to force those bodies into willingly
perpetuating the cycle, or subjectivation, of the product that is being created.
Videogame production is both a body and an assemblage. On the one hand,
it is a generalized apparatus that can facilitate becomings between technical
and nontechnical production bodies and the capitalist socius, has its own
agencements and contours, and has its own productive agenda. On the other
hand, videogame production has its own dynamic intensities that it is constantly tapping the molecular bodies within it to try and make sense of chaos
(Grosz, 2008).

By referring to "passion," I am taking it to mean a strong inclination
towards certain activities over others that acts as an agent of influence regarding choices, relationship-building, or pursuance of certain paths of education
or vocational training (Murnieks, Mosakowski, and Cardon, 2012). Passion
regarding videogames takes a few forms. Being committed to fully experiencing the depth and complexity that a certain game offers, spending a majority
of free time playing certain games and forming social bonds within the game
to other players or even to nonplayer characters, or referencing, participating
in, or creating unremunerated content for a game all constitute examples of
"passion" for videogames. This segues into "passion" regarding videogame
production quite well and explains the methodology by which recruitment-
via-passion is so insidious. As Murnieks, Mosakowski, and Cardon (2012)
say, "passion" can be a reason for choosing a certain vocation.

THE OPERATIONALIZATION OF PASSION

To start, I want to think through the base form of emotionality in videogame
production and how emotion, compounded with how the capitalist socius
creates cultural markers, creates an assemblage where passion, exploitation,
cultural markers, and autopoietic function all intersect to create the scene
where passion can become readily operationalized and used as fuel for the
process of videogame production.

When we talk about emotion, it is important to draw a distinction in *how*
we speak about it. Especially in how emotion interacts and contours the
assemblage that we are interested in talking about. The ways and means by
which intersections are made regarding emotion is important. It is important
to this book to make clear that "structuration" in the sense of Giddens's
(1984) work has its place, but needs careful consideration. For Giddens,
structuration sought a middle-ground between molar and molecular societal
analyses, meaning that Giddens was looking for something that foregrounded
individual biological actors. Structuration sees an immovable intersection

between "actor" and "structure" that can be pinpointed to determine some deeper truth, or some deeper rationale for the interaction. It is exactly this determinism and rigidity that renders this sort of ontological turn ultimately useless for this type of work except for understanding how passion and videogame production intersect. Structuration seeks an innate link between actor and structure, meaning that, if we adhere to structuration, cruel optimism is now forced to take on an innate emotional tone that we know is not always the case. While emotion can certainly *be* a driving force behind cruel optimism and cruelly optimistic collocation to an object, it is not the generalizable structure that Giddens is seeking. Structuration seeks to generalize how emotion is invested in situations and bodies, meaning that every action, thought, concept, interaction, etc. made within certain material-discursive boundaries automatically takes on a tone of emotion. This action, if anything, does not distribute emotionality but instead homogenizes it and assumes that each body that undergoes a set of actions, interactions, etc. are automatically meant to *feel* a certain way. This project cannot abide that sort of generalized play with emotion because of how granular and molecular this project's focus is. Deleuze and Guattari are not searching for any deeper meaning than a set of interactions, for those interactions *are* the meaning. Nothing hidden or latent; just purely interaction and actant. Resch (1992) says of Deleuze and Guattari's steps towards antistructuration:

> For Deleuze, ontology is difference: the essence of all being is plural, productive, and devoid of deeper unity or meaning. Behind every thing or idea there are differences, yet behind difference there is nothing. By ontologizing the concept of difference, Deleuze seeks to escape from the labyrinth of absence and presence that envelops discursive practices, and it is this illusion of absence that serves as the (anti-) foundation of his thought. (230)

My use of "passion" and cruel optimism as connective tissues is not an articulation of a place where "actor" (body of some sort) meets "agent" (in this case, videogame production). The main intersection of agent and structure that I am looking at here is that of "passion" and "recruitment" within videogame production and why this exact coordinate is so important to keep in mind when thinking through how the capitalist socius overlays onto videogame production and the ultimate goal of both: autopoiesis.

Before discussing how the capitalist socius overlays onto videogame production, it is important to talk about "videogame production" and recruitment methods used in videogame production. Both of these topics present important differences from other forms of media production that are often overlooked or misunderstood. Videogame production in and of itself represents a production media where both professional (e.g., on payroll for an indie company or a triple-A company) and nonprofessional (e.g., hobbyists, hackers, modders, and one-person studios) videogame producers can see widespread success. Not only is there a plethora of low-cost or free videogame production tools, such as Twine, RPG Maker, GameMaker, Unity, and Unreal, but there are also multitudes of videogame production books that can help developers craft new, out-of-the-box ideas (e.g., Isbister's *How Games Move Us*, 2017; Rusch's *Making Deep Games*, 2017; and Flanagan and Nissenbaum's *Values at Play in Digital Games*, 2016). Additionally, platforms such as Steam, the Epic Store, and itch.io allow creators of any stripe to distribute their games to a potentially huge audience, both for profit and not-for-profit.

Unlike other media production apparatuses such as filmmaking or photography, videogame production's unique kit of production platforms and distribution platforms create an environment where success can be experienced by anyone in accordance with neoliberal ideology like allowing the monetary or cultural success of a game to determine its validity. This fundamental decentralization of a definitive, defined body of videogame producers that one must go through to experience commercial success creates an environment where "success" and the ability to "make it" without having institutional backing is ultimately in the hands of whomever is making the game. It also presents an environment where certain worker protections such as unionization require much more thought, planning, and action to even take root.

Videogame production in any form covets time devoted to a project as a way of gauging the amount of passion being given to a book. Videogame production's labor schedules and pipelines in many triple-A and indie development studios are created around expected periods of crunch (Dyer-Witheford and DePeuter, 2006), or periods of work where workers are expected to put in sometimes as much as 16 hours of work a day for an extended period. Additionally, recruitment methods for videogame production at all corporate levels (community management, quality assurance, programming, art and sound, etc.) rely on, first, appealing to a potential worker's passion for playing videogames, and then exploiting that passion. Cruel optimism can be used to describe the cycle that videogame production perpetuates. Videogame production is touted as a "do what you love" endeavor (Tokumitsu, 2014) where, the more labor you put into the apparatus of production, the more opportunities you have for advancement. Todd Howard's rise to fame with Bethesda is often peddled out as a case study when informally talking about passion and meritocratic advancement in videogames. As I spoke about in the first chapter, Todd Howard is one of the more well-known presences in videogame production who presents his foray into production as him allowing his passion for videogames to lead him, him being dogged and determined to make a name for himself (Game Informer, 2011), and him being rewarded accordingly. Meritocracy, seemingly, did not fail Todd Howard in the way that it has failed many, many other production workers in the form of unfulfilled promises to hire on contingent workers, provide more stability for contingent workers, and advance "diverse" people into positions of power within video-game production (Paul, 2018). Cruel optimism in videogame production sees young bodies that are passionate about playing videogames or interacting with videogame culture being recruited, and then their passion is turned into a subjectivation tool to force them into accepting periods of crunch (Bulut, 2015; Johnson, 2013a) because they want to advance or feel obligated to want to advance. By distinguishing how labor differs from general media production, it is possible to understand in a more meaningful way what possible intensities, contours, and potentials videogame production has, and how the capitalist socius preys on the potentiality therein.

Deleuze and Guattari's conception of a "Body without Organs" (Deleuze and Guattari, 1983), or BwO, presents a way of exploring these potentialities. It is not enough to describe one production company or one worker or one type of game as a way of characterizing all of videogame production. Instead, it is important to understand the entanglement that each worker, each game, each production company has with similar bodies; the potential becomings of, and intensities present within, each body, technical or nontechnical, present an entirely new set of possibilities. BwO provides a way of touching and interacting with multiplicative possible becomings within videogame production by not isolating any one part of videogames or production and asking it to stand on its own merits, or to speak for an entire sector:

> Deleuze and Guattari's description of the Body without Organs (BwO), which is invoked to demonstrate the insufficiency of describing bodies and the notion of subjectivity in terms of components (organs) possessed by those bodies. To know what a body can be is not as simple as knowing what it contains. Instead of organs, bodies "can be occupied, populated only by intensities." (Reider & Halm, 2020)

It is important to understand, first, the deeper interactions under the shiny veneer of videogame production, and second how BwO works to allow us to see interconnectedness within actors in the apparatus of videogame production. Passion, as I have said before, is the connective tissue that is operating within the becomings I am interested in in videogame production. Passion comes in many forms: passion for playing games, experiencing games (e.g., watching eSports, Twitch, Let's Plays), creating games, hacking games, modding games. Each of these forms of passion has its own affective attachments that the passion-holder (in this, a potential production worker) defines for themselves. The interaction of passion and recruitment, then, operates at many different intensities that speak to each potential worker's embodied experiences that shape their own passion. Passion asks of the passion-holder to perform a form of autopoiesis (Varela and Maturana, 1972) to maintain that passion. The goal is to keep being fulfilled by the activity at hand. But to attain that goal and to fend off burnout or loss of interest, the passion-holder must invest themselves in different and varied activities within the culture to continue feeling justified in having a passion for this thing. For example, if someone is passionate about watching Let's Plays, they likely have a variety of Twitch or YouTube channels that they follow that produce different content; one may be a YouTube channel specializing in scary games, another may be a Twitch channel that specializes in speed runs or fighting games. The thing that keeps the passion for experiencing games fresh is that these channels are constantly producing new content that, when the passion-holder interacts with them, creates a spatiotemporal bubble where every interaction, every mouse-click or button push, every thought, every affect that occurs is specific to that spatiotemporal moment. Passion, then, is not an amorphous blob that engulfs a concept. Instead, it is akin to a chain of paper clips: each paper clip added to the chain of passion represents an intensity or becoming that is personal to that moment. It is self-defining, and it is nothing more or less than the affect within that spatiotemporal moment anchoring itself to the previous spatiotemporal moment to continue the chain and continue the autopoietic nature of passion.

If passion is this multifaceted, molecular daisy-chain of becomings, then recruitment must make sense of that passion, and understand how best to insert itself into the paper clip chain so as not to break the chain, but to deterritorialize and reterritorialize flows of work (e.g., creating knowledge capital). Deleuze and Guattari (1980) refer to wasps attempting to copulate with orchids as an example of how certain interactions or becomings can be thought of as ways of de- and reterritorializing, or as a rhizome. This metaphor applies neatly to videogame production. If the goal of the capitalist socius is to achieve autopoiesis, continue subjectivating bodies so that they are amenable to knowledge production, and to have value surpluses of knowledge, and the goal of videogame production is to continue existing within the socius and benefiting from its structure, then the way that recruitment must operate is akin to the wasp and orchid. The orchid mimics and lures the wasp to it to assist in reproduction (what Deleuze and Guattari refer to as a signifying element): images of having fun while you work, doing what you love, the cultural clout of working in videogames. We can understand this beaconing as recruitment, and we can see where cruel optimism starts to take root. The fervor with which the wasp attempts to copulate with the orchid can be seen as passion, while each thrust, rub, or death can be seen as the interlinking passion paper clips. The action of breeding can be seen as the cruelly optimistic aspect of this dance: the wasp is tricked into relying on its subjectivated nature to try and copulate and reproduce with the orchid. The pollen that is transferred from orchid to wasp is the capitalist socius exploiting that passion and the signifying elements that appeal to the worker by embedding subjectivating elements into that paper clip chain. These interactions are forming a map of possible intensities and becomings between worker, knowledge production, and passion, possible entries and exits that exist purely to accommodate new forms of passion, new forms of production, new platforms, new cruelly optimistic attachments, and new ways of interaction between these elements.

The Capitalist Socius, Videogame Production, Integrated World Capitalism

Deleuze and Guattari (1983) provide a way of contextualizing how capitalism, as a social construct, came to be through characterizing the historical transformations of property ownership and ruling relations as first a "savage" socius, then as a "despotic" socius, and finally, as a "capitalist" socius. The savage socius was organized around tribal relations: bodies are marked in ceremonies, which then insert those bodies into "clans" from which products are traced. Land is claimed by tribes; that land is credited with production of materials in a symbiotic relation to the clan itself. As societies set down roots, and land claims became more routinized, the despotic socius formed. As land is amassed, warred over, and conquered, clan-land production loses its claim and instead empire-rule is the way of the world. As more land is acquired and mixed together, single-clan claims for production are no longer honored, and thus a new attribution model needed to be made. In the despotic socius, this became the despot, or the divine father of the people over whom he ruled. Production (in this case, production means land seizure as well as actual, material production) is attributed to the despot. The capitalist socius is a complete departure from the savage and despotic sociuses that Deleuze and Guattari discussed in *Anti-Oedipus* (1983). Whereas the savage and despotic sociuses were concerned with acculturating their citizens, and establishing hierarchies of dominance, the capitalist socius's main goal is production, and it relies on outside means to overload bodies with information, or overcode, and to force those bodies into willingly perpetuating the cycle, or subjectivation, of the product that is being created. I am speaking of videogame production in relation to the capitalist socius in this section, not as a competitor or separate entity, but as a companion to it. The capitalist socius overloads bodies with cultural markers regarding videogames (they're fun, they're cool, when you make them all you do is play at work, etc.) to overcode those bodies into becoming productive bodies that must adhere to the idea that videogames, and videogame production, have to be the way that they are, and must be guarded, lest their form of subjectivation that is allowing them to survive in capitalist society becomes threatened.

By quantifying production in the sphere of videogames, the capitalist socius creates a space where the inherent purpose of the bodies that work within it is to connect deterritorialized flows of labor, meaning that instead of working toward a community's communal interest, like in the savage and despotic sociuses, workers are subjectivated to overproduce and not expect to take part in the bounty of overproduction. The excess that is produced is not redistributed equally to workers, but instead is hoarded by a select few bodies. This hoarding is done in a bid to further strip the identities of the bodies working within the capitalist socius and to create bodies that are conditioned to produce, expect little in the way of recompense, but always have the proverbial carrot on a string of "one day you too could own your own studio or make your own game, you just have to work harder."

Peticca-Harris et al. (2015) talk about the extreme working conditions of the videogame production process by examining two very well-known whistle-blowing blog posts from spouses of game developers at triple-A studios: the EA Spouse blog and the Rockstar Spouse blog. Both describe long periods of crunch, abusive management, and in-fighting due to stress that the spouses of the blog-writers endured. Burnout, depression, and health- and family-related problems are all very real possibilities of working in the industry (Johnson, 2013; Dyer-Witheford and de Peuter, 2006; Bulut, 2014 and 2015; Williams, 2013b and 2018). These conditions are due in large part to the working expectations of videogame production. Lionhead Studios's buy-out by Microsoft and subsequent shuttering is just one example of hundreds where the capitalist socius acquires a potentially productive body and attempts to regulate it, but does not account for the molecular differences in desiring-production of each worker, and the entity's desiring-productive circuit board over all. In this case, Lionshead failed to produce adequately subjectivizable bodies to do the work that Microsoft wanted which, in turn, failed to produce the value surplus of knowledge that Microsoft needed to consider the acquisition valuable.

The bodies at work creating and developing videogames are not the only bodies being remade by the videogame industry. In The Three Ecologies (1989), Guattari discusses the concept of integrated world capitalism (IWC), which Pindar and Sutton, in the translator's notes, define as:

> Postindustrial capitalism—which Guattari calls Integrated World Capitalism (IWC) is delocalized and deterritorialized to such an extent that is impossible to locate the source of its power. IWC's most potent weapon for achieving social control without violence is the mass media. (4)

In the case of videogame production and consumption, the television set, as Pindar and Sutton reference, is not the point of entrance: instead, we must look at the global networks behind the videogames we consume. In addition to the devastatingly stressful environments that videogame production takes place in, a good portion of that work is outsourced, contributing to further job instability and precarity. Paul Hyman (2008) examines how the outsourcing practices of videogame art were an early harbinger of things to come. The company he profiles, THQ (today known as THQNordic), is a multibillion dollar triple-A videogame producer that refers to outsourcing as "distributed development." Hyman references THQ having outsourced 20–25% of their art asset development in 2008, whereas today they outsource somewhere around 80% of their art asset development. Their in-house production is now primarily game systems, proprietary art assets, and marketing/branding. THQ's rampant outsourcing speaks to both the nature of the capitalist socius and of the videogame production process: what you keep in-house will end up costing you more than outsourcing. The majority of the art assets that THQ's internal developers outsource are to developing countries with burgeoning tech sectors like India, and increasingly Eastern Europe; this means that, for what would cost these internal developers millions of dollars to develop in-house, they can outsource for it to be developed for a fraction of that price.

In addition to the physical labor the bodies in question in videogame production engage in, the immaterial labor invested in games is another important aspect of IWC. Lazzarato defines immaterial labor as "the labor that produces the informational and cultural content of the commodity" (1996, 132). Constance Steinkuehler (2006) wrote about the international distribution and privilege of play in Lineage. She profiles the "Chinese farmer"[1] in Lineage II:

> For-profit companies in China were hiring people to play Lineage II for virtual currency in exchange for real-world pay. The practice continues largely unchecked today, and the attending controversy has nothing but intensified. [. . .] As best as I can piece together, Chinese adena farmers normally work 12-hour shifts . . . with two people to each computer so that the in-game character they share is always online. Typically, they must collect 300,000 adena per shift in exchange for their daily wage of about US $3. It may not sound like much, but compared to China's average yearly income of US $316, it's rather lucrative work.

Julian Dibbell (2016) built on this work, addressing the issues of whether paid gold farmers are players, and whether unpaid farmers are employees, echoing many of the same questions that have been asked in modding discourse (Kuchlich, 2005; Sotamaa, 2007; Gallagher et al., 2017; Lauteria, 2012).

The immaterial labor taking place in both of these pieces further highlights the world-wide precarity of videogame culture: "playbour" (Kuchlich, 2005) takes place as a means of making a living in third-world countries while this work is sold to Western players for inflated prices; players who have the means can benefit and perpetuate the necessity of this labor by buying the gold and items these people farm, which gives those players an inherent advantage over other players.

Dibbell and Steinkuehler don't consider the mechanisms of discipline that gold-farming sweatshops incorporate that further subjectivate the bodies laboring in those spaces: the spaces in which these bodies farm virtual gold resemble the development areas of many triple-A game studios. There is no sense of privacy, and the "fun" that is associated with playing a videogame is absent in much the same way as other unrecognized areas of videogame production: QA testing suffering burnout and job instability (Bulut, 2014; Williams, 2013), and community managers being expected to respond to community issues 24/7 (Kerr and Kelleher, 2015), to name a few examples. Both farmers and videogame production workers labor under conditions that do not value privacy: no partitions or cubicles, all the workers work in the open and are monitored by management; they have quotas to meet, and they work grueling hours to meet those quotas (see: Webster, 2018 for a discussion about Red Dead Redemption II's developers working 100-hour weeks to finish production). Both workspaces have a sense of panoptic control: the bodies laboring in these environments are being monitored, and should their work not be satisfactory, they can be replaced as quickly as they were hired.

Subjectivation Station(s)

Lazzarato, in Signs and Machines (2014), says that capitalism

> reveals a twofold cynicism: the "humanist" cynicism of assigning us individuality and pre-established roles (worker, consumer, unemployed, man/woman, artist, etc.) in which individuals are necessarily alienated; and the "dehumanizing" cynicism of including us in an assemblage that no longer distinguishes between human and nonhuman, subject and object, or words and things. (13)

While capitalism is complicit in perpetuating binaries by creating and maintaining the material properties of bodily normativity by linking things such as gender to colors, masculinity or femininity to clothes and hygiene products, and masculinity/femininity to sports, it also allows rampant cultural subjectivation in other strata. For example, in the videogame production process, hypermasculinity, antifeminism, and colonialism (white male saving a kingdom/town/woman from a nonhuman [read: nonwhite] threat) are common storylines in videogames. But the question remains: how, and why, are these tropes perpetuated, even in games that are supposed to be progressive and inclusive?

I want to start by addressing the binary of production/antiproduction that Guattari references (1996). Antiproduction accounts for the things that are not getting made. Guattari refers to cinema as a medium of "transference, Oedipus, and castration" (235), meaning that cinema produces cultural markers by which bodies in modern society become subjectivated to value certain standards of beauty, products, religious forms, and other marks of enculturation so as to make these things profitable and able to be monetized. In other words, Guattari alludes to cinema as being a trend-setting affair. It creates the "cool" things that drive supply and demand. The case can be made, too, that videogames operate in much the same way as cinema insofar as they both subjectivate consumers to value certain products, bodies, and forms over others, and create value systems that other media incorporate, adhere to, or run the risk of failing. The value systems that triple-A game production values and perpetuates are tropes of antifemininity, hypermasculinity, colonialism, etc.

Videogame production processes subsist on, historically, keeping games that focus on personal, affective experiences out of mainstream production culture and instead, selling iteratively different content to quantifiable bodies (e.g., war games such as Call of Duty, Battlefield, Halo, FIFA, etc. being marketed mostly to male, 18–35, heterosexual, white bodies). Current videogame production processes, though, are beginning to understand and recognize that affective and emotionally investing games can be monetized (Rusch, 2017; Isbister, 2017). So, whereas intimate, timely experiences that were rendered in videogame form used to be prevalent only in DIY and non-professional spaces (Fisher and Harvey, 2013), the capitalist socius has begun to develop the tools to consume and repurpose these game types in service of capitalism. In professional videogame development spaces, the bodies creating these affective experiences and attachments have not changed, either; in fact, the bodies in these spaces have stayed much the same (Weststar and Legault, 2017; Williams, 2018; Fisher and Harvey, 2013). This has fostered an increasingly toxic and predatory work environment in which videogame production workers must labor under subjectivation regimes of not only being ok with creating and perpetuating antifeminine, hypermasculine, colonialist, and antihomo/transsexual media, but now also affectively and emotionally predatory media as well, further instantiating the dehumanizing cynicism that Lazzarato talks about by expecting workers to cede any moral judgments or objections to books.

The cultural spaces that videogames inhabit have long been an "old boy's club" (Johnson, 2013a; Dyer-Witheford & Sharman, 2005) in which women's bodies are marginalized—thought of as weak, needing to be rescued—while men perpetuate hypermasculine tropes of killing and colonizing (Paaßen, Morgenroth, Stratemeyer, 2016). Women are attacked and their validity, personal and professional, is called into question (Fisher, 2015; Kerr and Kelleher, 2015). They are ignored as audiences; thought to just be " . . . vacant pinups to be ogled or irrelevant sidekicks to be tolerated, and real women [are] annoying interlopers to be bullied" (Fisher, 2015). Even in instances of attempted diversification (Fisher and Harvey, 2013), women's professional wants and needs are often ignored and downplayed. A prescient example of this is the recent controversy surrounding Bobby Kotick, Activision Blizzard, and the overwhelming antifeminism that has taken root and propagated freely. I will speak more about these events towards the end of this text, but it is important to make mention of them here considering how important it is to understand the insidious aspect of subjectivation in videogame production that has historically required nonmale bodies to engage in active renegotiation of gender in order to fit in.

Videogame production spaces are no better than most other cultural spaces concerning videogames where gender inclusivity and diversity are concerned. Johnson (2013a) talks about hypermasculinity and the "boy's club" mentality of videogame production as something that:

some men . . . lamented . . . , [but] many of their explanations centered on the idea that the gender imbalance is simply due to the fact that more men than women apply for jobs in the industry. [. . .] other men offered a clearer window into the sexism of the digital play industry, explaining, for example, that "girls" often do not have "the right ideas" when it comes to games but that it "looks good" for a developer to employ "some girls." (579)

Not only are the culture and working spaces of videogame production hypermasculine and homogeneous, but that gender imbalance is what allows the industry to function in the highly racialized and gendered manner that it does. The temporal dimensions of the highly gendered and racialized nature of production spaces are not locked in splintered, nonconnected events; the subjectivation of workers to include tropes that perpetuate dominance of one body type over another exists as a corporate culture and climate, not as one or two peoples' opinions that somehow manage to sneak into games. From conceptual stages through creation, conscious aesthetic choices determine the continuity or usurping of hypermasculinity in both the production spaces, and in the products themselves (Johnson, 2013a).

Change in these realms does not happen with any urgency. Videogame production spaces are risk-averse and are often so locked to capitalistic production cycles that even if a studio wanted to rehabilitate its culture, often that cannot happen due to the nature of stagnation that the capitalist socius favors. Simply put, slow, incremental changes to videogame IPs and genres are prized over innovation and newness, both in triple-A production spaces and indie production spaces (Johnson, 2013b). This perspective speaks to the Guattarian (1989) notion of heterogenesis as being

> an active, immanent singularization of subjectivity, as opposed to a transcendent, universalizing and reductionist homogenization . . . an expression of desire, of a becoming that is always in the process of adapting, transforming and modifying itself in relation to its environment. (95n49)

Heterogeny and iterative design are locked together in videogame production because they are part and parcel of what Guattari referred to with cinema (Guattari, 1996): videogame production is an enculturation endeavor and is responsible for subjectivating large sectors of the population. Capitalism has encouraged videogame production to target certain audiences, readily subjectivize them to accept certain bodily, racial, and sexual portrayals as valid. Any attempt to break with those readily recognizable tropes would mean that the entire industry would have to radically reformat not only itself, but to whom it is marketing or risk the entire medium crumbling in on itself from alienating faithful consumers. This is, again, seen played out in the culture of videogame production spaces. The bodies at work creating the subjectivizing material have themselves been subjectivized to some degree into accepting the validity of only certain bodies for the medium, and, whether consciously or not, that subjectivization has embedded itself in workplace cultures that actively favor (mostly white) straight men for meritocratic purposes such as promotion (D'Anastasio, 2018).

Large developers encourage heterogeneity throughout their studios. If the production processes and workflows are similar, it is easier to identify where and when a system is breaking down so that it can be rectified (Neilson and Rossiter, 2005; Brooks, 1974; Crowley et al., 2010). If the workspaces are similar, it follows that, as more heterogenic elements are incorporated into the life of a studio, even games from different genres will start to emulate one another's systems and become mixed-genre media. And just as the games become more similar, the bodies that make those games are expected to become more similar. This is where the tropes of hypermasculinity and anti-feminism and anti-individualism start to become apparent. Dyer-Witheford & de Peuter (2006) state that "for many, the initially enjoyable aspects of work in digital play mutate into a linchpin of exploitative and exclusionary practices, including exclusion based upon gender."

Gender moderation is another aspect of production culture that contributes to the precarity of videogame production and perpetuation of negative tropes.

Prescott and Bogg (2011) find that gender segregation is still happening in triple-A production spaces, and that women who do enter the industry must, at least partially, renegotiate their gender identity in order to fit in better with male coworkers (Johnson, 2013a and 2018). Johnson (2018) outlines how, if they do not do the work of renegotiating, they run the risk of being accused of being "fake gamers" (Taylor, Jenson, and de Castell, 2009; D'Anastasio, 2018) and have their passion called into question. This then calls the validity of their attachments into question, which, as Johnson (2013a) says, can make nonmen even more susceptible to their passions being operationalized to further extract overwork by means of not only questioning cultural fit, but also deeply held affective bonds towards those objects of cruel optimism. This further demonstrates an unwillingness on the part of male production workers to accept alternate forms of passion to their own, alternate forms of bodies, and what those bodies are capable of.

The act of renegotiating gender in videogame production spaces becomes an act of subsistence rather than the more modern act of subversion that queer theory has attempted to recast it as (Butler, 1990; Halberstam, 2011; Munoz, 1999). In modern culture, gender fluidity is recognized and is becoming more and more accepted, and bodies are free to express their gender how they see fit. In processes of capitalist subjectivation though, nonmale bodies, or bodies that are not willing to perform the necessary gender renegotiating to become-male (Guattari, 1996) become a hindrance. In an interview Johnson (2013a) conducted, he was able to extract a clear look at gender in the videogame production process:

> other men offered a clearer window into the sexism of the digital play industry, explaining, for example, that "girls" often do not have "the right ideas" when it comes to games but that it "looks good" for a developer to employ "some girls." (579)

The necessity of women to renegotiate their femininity, or to become-male, to be taken seriously and valued in the videogame production process presents a very troubling look at how gender is performed in these spaces, and how videogame production's workplace culture has come to recognize only one certain type of body as acceptably axiomatizable.

SURVIVING TO WIN, AND WINNING TO SURVIVE

In the case of biological bodies, capitalist socius, and videogame production bodies, the body that is experiencing autopoiesis is experiencing a continual rebirth and renewal of structures of investment. In the case of autopoiesis in videogame production, the renewal of structures of investment means that, as old production workers or disaffected workers or workers who are underperforming are removed from videogame production, new bodies with fresh passion are recruited and subjectivized. If the body is not experiencing autopoiesis, it degrades, the systems and infrastructure break down, and the body eventually ceases to exist. Thinking of autopoiesis as "the autoreproductive capacity of a structure or ecosystem" (Guattari and Stéphane, 2006, 93), it becomes easier to imagine that the overarching goal of both the capitalist socius and of the videogame production process is simply to survive. They also seek to continue to create capital, perpetuate the tropes creating the capital, and to continue to subjectivate and consume bodies and ideas to create workers that will continue creating capital. These entities' goals of achieving maintainable autopoiesis play a large part in the continuity of the stereotypes and tropes of bodies that characterize videogame production and general capitalism. To subsist, the capitalist socius and videogame production both have to actively work to create new methods of subjectivation in areas outside of their consumptive radiuses.

Ergin Bulut (2015) profiles how utopian rhetorics of "fun," and "playbour" and "grassroots creativity efforts" regarding how working in the videogame production process have been utilized to draw in talented individuals. What the rhetorics do not address are the precarity and insidious nature of keeping a job in this industry. The company that Bulut (2015) profiles was once an independent videogame production space which was bought out by a conglomerate due to failing finances; when the first company was bought out, its entire workflow changed from making games that were interesting to them, to making games on the whims of "stock markets and decision-making processes at the corporate level, putting the developers 'in limbo, waiting to see what's gonna happen' as the management would tell [Bulut]" (195). Eventually, the once-independent company was deskilled and financialized into the workflow similar to what Johnson talked about regarding incrementalization, and what Guattari referred to as heterogenesis. Most importantly Bulut noticed that, in addition to the steady decline of employed workers and the burnout experienced by all levels of workers, the corporate culture of the company became more and more divisive, exclusionary, and divided. The "above-the-line" workers (senior developers, book managers, CFO/CIT/C__) started to treat other workers in mechanized ways. Nothing except workflow was important, and "the introduction of book managers created conflict since book managers were seen as 'cracking the whip across the board'" (Bulut, 2014). Bulut noticed, too, that as deskilling was occurring, the below-line workers complained of having to manage each other instead of producing the content they had been hired to produce. This peer-management went for such things as code documentation, documenting changes and edits in art assets, and even keeping peers motivated to actually do these things. The precarity of peer-management, in addition to the sudden subjectivization of workers' bodies to become "mechanical" and process-driven, financialization of the company, and deskilling of the workforce produced a negative feedback loop. For the few women that were present in Bulut's 2.4 years of fieldwork, most of them expressed increasing feelings of inadequacy and depression due to peer pressure to "do better, be better, and get better things done," and "stop letting emotions rule everything and just do the work" (198).

Push Meets Shove: Precarity in Our System of Autopoietic Videogame Production

I want to spend a moment addressing cruel optimism again in collocation with and in the capitalist socius. The way that Berlant (and I) character- ize cruel optimism is that those experiencing cruel optimism has some sort of indentured attachment to an object, affect, or concept. This means that, without proximity to and access to (or, rather, striving *to* access) the object/ affect/concept in question, the person experiencing cruel optimism is suffer- ing some sort of deficiency. Within the system of autopoietic subjectivation that the videogame production relies on to subsist, it is not so much the act of attachment that is the problem, though. Nor is it the act of collocation. In fact, the material-discursive circumstances *of* cruel optimism really are not the cruel part. Yes, we could consider parts of it cruel in that collocation requires entanglement with toxic elements such as the operationalization of passion. But if that is the case, cruel optimism should perhaps be referred to as toxic optimism? The act of collocation is not the problem at hand that needs a slightly deeper understanding, at least not in videogame production.

Instead, I posit that it is the act of collocation to the *object;* the com- bination of attachment and the attached: this vaunted, valorized, painful, cutting image of what success is and what "being productive" means. In videogame production, this image of productivity (and hyperproductivity) are laser-focused. If you are not suffering for your art a la Mike Epps's 2006 tirade about culture fit and expecting to work 60 hours a week at least, then, in the current zeitgeist of videogame production, you are not successful, you are not passionate enough, and you are not deserving of the artificially sacred spaces in videogame production. This, then, links back to the idea of precarity that we have discussed already. This artificial scarcity of jobs/ places in videogame production act as an active interference with the BwO's continual becomings. Libidinal energy is supposed to flow throughout the body in roils and lines of flight that continually contour and recontour the assemblages and agencements that we can observe the Body in. But, when we introduce artificial inflation to the Body, all of a sudden, the roil and chaotic movement of libidinal energy is no longer true. It becomes choked and it becomes inauthentic, and then the becomings that Deleuze and Guattari make such pains to outline as these objects of potentiality and schizorevolution are rendered ineffective and constipated. The artificial inflation of space within the BwO allows for antiproductive energy to permeate and roil against the libidinal energy. This is where the precarity starts to manifest in our day-to-day embodied lives. And not only manifest, but bloom and become encompassing. Going back to the aspect of cruel optimism in this equation, all of a sudden it becomes clear that the collocative factor, and the *need* to collocate next to a set of potentially toxic elements, exacerbates the precarities that we encounter due to what we are collocating against.

Cruel optimism's wide-reaching theoretical impact is important. But even when figuring out how and where cruelly optimistic collocation exists within the capitalist socius, there are possibilities to be generative with where we locate problematicity. A lot of the precarity that we see in videogame production does not come directly from cruel optimism; it comes from the attachments and entanglements *surrounding* the cruel optimism, and the subjectivation systems in place that direct us to those points of collocation. The subjectivation: the expectations of hyperproductivity; the performativity of "passion" and "machismo." This is where precarity starts to appear, and these areas are where videogame production slips through less granular, less careful theorization, which is why we need to think possibly beyond precarity in the singular and instead think of precari*ties*, perhaps.

NOTE

1. "Chinese farmer" in this context references a person, often of Asian descent, who works in sweatshop conditions killing in-game enemies over and over again to harvest gold that is then sold to other players for real-world money.

Chapter 3

Toward a Theorization
of *Precarities*

My focus through this book has been on trying to find ways to reformat and remediate how we, as scholarly activists, perceive and talk through precarity. I want to posit a formative (re)theorization of "precarity" to "precarit*ies*." The point in differentiating between "precarity" and "precarities" is that one is a catch-all term to describe possible instances of, well, precarity. As the literature in the first chapter describes, "precarity" as a theorized concept spans a number of circumstances, attributions, situations, etc. and is catalyzed by, contained within, and signified by a number of affects, uncontrollable floes, and redirections within production, and whims of late-stage capitalism. What the conceptions of precarity that were covered in the first chapter do not account for, and what the conceptualization of how the capitalist socius overlays onto videogame production in the second chapter can't account for are highlighted by my informants from fieldwork will speak about in this chapter: misattribution, nonspecificity, and one-size-fits-all description. In order for the goal of this book to be realized, groundwork needs to be done toward a formative theorization of *precarities*. There are intersections and entanglements between humans, conditions of labor, and extenuating circumstances that are not addressed by business psychology, organizational communication, critical media studies, Deleuzoguattarian studies, or game studies that must be addressed. Precarity as a concept covers a lot of theoretical ground, and it gives scholars a way of talking through tumultuous working and living conditions without having to identify or engage with the underlying issues that are causing what they deem "precarious." This book, however, *needs* to engage with these issues. Therefore, it is important to move towards a multifaceted, multidimensional theorization of *precarities*.

The previous two chapters provided important definitional work that enable this chapter to exist, including what passion is, how it can be operationalized, what precarity is and is not, how cloudy and one-size-fits-all its definitions are, and how the capitalist socius works to subjectivize workers to create and maintain autopoiesis. The second is an understanding of how, under these concepts, cruel optimism is working to lubricate and allow for these issues to exist and propagate by way of the subjectivation that is already occurring within the capitalist socius to create workers who adhere to strict workflows to alleviate potential hiccups in the process of production. The end product is an ironclad system of subjectivation that accounts for bodies both organic and inorganic and their interconnectedness on multiple different planes. The end product also accounts for, and in fact readily consumes and monetizes, anticapitalist movements. These considerations still amount to and encourage an umbrella understanding of "precarity," whereas in reality, these issues are granular, intricate, and personal, and therefore deserve the type of theorization that allows for that kind of care and understanding to be given to further understanding how to *fix* those issues. The situation that I keep coming back to after talking to people in the industry who I have developed a rapport with, rereading interviews I have conducted, and revisiting relations I have established through this work is that precarity is not simply attributional. Definitional work around precarity also has to account for how workers speak about, manage, feel, and establish ontologies in regard to a system that generates precarity for its workers. This means that, in addition to just identifying what situations may be precarious, we also need to understand the in/organic body's understanding of those material-discursive circumstances.

This chapter is here to help renegotiate and realign how we talk about precarity as an videogame production community, how we talk about pre-carit*ies* in terms of labor negotiation, and how we understand the people who are actively engaged in these precarities. In essence, precarities are the ways by which workers negotiate, verbalize, manage, feel, and interact with the system of videogame production. The system itself perpetuates the cyclical aspects of dehumanizing, casualizing, and operationalizing workers and their work, and the multiplicative processes by which workers negotiate those interactions embody what I call precarit*ies*.

PARTICIPANT INFORMATION: GRANULAR
NEEDS, CAREFUL CONSIDERATIONS

In this chapter, I want to make use of some ethnographic fieldwork I have done over the span of my academic career. I have had the opportunity of inter-viewing and embedding with approximately 52 US videogame production workers over my academic career, ranging from studio managers to quality assurance workers to sound designers to art/asset designers to coders. The scope of studios that I have been able to observe and take part in range from triple-A studios to indie studios to just someone's living room. But regard-less of where they are working, each of their granular, embodied experiences are incredibly important to this book and to the points that I am articulating through this book. That being said, not all of them are comfortable with their experiences being discussed in long form in the way that this chapter calls for. In order to respect their wishes, maintain their privacy, and still give credence to their experiences, I want to preface this chapter by saying that, while I may not invoke their experiences by name, the sentiments that they have shared with me helped me to formulate the ideas that I discuss in this chapter around multiplicative precarities.

Some very basic stats from my research of how participant responses broke down by the aspects of precarities that I talk about. 47 of 52 informants reported feeling some form of trauma from working in videogames, be it anecdotal, medical/diagnosed, still processing, or resolved. Reported traumas ranged from nagging feelings of being used for their labor over long periods of time to very physical, very real traumatic events that happened in their studios, around their studios, or collocated with the times in which they were imbricated with game creation that left an affective mark on that creation experience.

51 of 52 informants specifically talked about times when they were ren-dered vulnerable due to work, due to trauma, or due to having to negotiate risk. The importance of this facet of precarity, though, is that vulnerability was not always a negative-coded affect. Participants talked at length about feelings of safety and being seen in their vulnerability. They talked about partners, therapists, friends, family, coworkers, even pets that made them feel like they could let their guards down and express how they were truly feeling without fear of reprisal or being made to feel like they did not belong. Some informants talked about these positive feelings of vulnerability alongside negative feelings of vulnerability, though. From my informants' stories, there is no clear good or bad discursivity to their experiences, nor is there an exact spatiotemporal, physical, embodied, or architectural common point to these experiences.

48 of 52 informants talked about how they understood risk as an element of being in a precarious situation and how they used support networks, self-efficacy, or professional resources such as financial advisers to offset, or redistribute, some of that risk so that the volatility of videogame production did not affect their ability to provide for loved ones. Of those 48, though, 41 talked about risk and redistribution in a similar way to how informants talked about vulnerability: it is not necessarily negative, or a burden. They talked about the grace that their family, partners, investors, and coworkers showed them to help them negotiate their relationship with risky behavior. Some also talked about the challenge of risk as being integral to them taking career steps

that they would not have otherwise such as starting their own studio, leaving their current studio, or leaving the type of role they historically had filled to do something else (e.g., sr. communications manager to jr. rigger in one instance). Again, there was no prevailing theme around whether or not risk and redistribution is inherently negative; participants recognized that there are negative aspects of risk, but the 41 that I invoke here acknowledge that, largely, they are not in this alone and that they have support networks that are there to help them navigate risk.

Going back to the discussion on Giddens and structuration, I want to highlight that the vast majority of the ethnographic work that I have done further enforces what Deleuze and Guattari (1983) are adamant about in antistructuration: interactions do not necessarily connote emotionality, and interactions should be taken as just that: a set of interactions that have their own innate sociodiscursive and ontological meanings. There is no deeper, more salacious, premeditated connotation to most interactions we see in videogame production. We are operating within an inherently late-stage capitalistic machination that needs so badly to dictate becomings and lines of flight that it aims to monetize capital in any way possible (physical, immaterial, knowledge, etc.). It also creates cultural markers that direct lines of subjectivation within the media to direct bodies towards certain paths of becoming that fit into the machinic logics of the system. It is *those* interactions we need to be concerned about, which arguably are not even interactions but Sisyphean boulders we, as videogame production workers, must roll uphill by way of exploiting our own passionate attachment to the medium. Hence why this section, my ethnographic work altogether, and especially these recontextualizations of general precarity into precarit*ies* heavily avoid dwelling on situational affect or reading into anything that my informants did not actually say. I adhere to Kamila Vizweswaran's *Feminist Ethnography* (1994) in many ways, and the aspect that I think is most important is that what your informants say is their truth, and while that truth may not meet your own sensibilities or experiences, it is truth and must be treated with the same diligence and respect that you would expect your own truth to be treated with.

INTRODUCING . . .

In this section, I want to take time to introduce six informants who, from the beginning of our relationships, have been very vocal that I am free to use their words in my work. Each of them have been part of my iterative writing process and have seen their individual contributions to this chapter and have given it their approval for how I talk about their experiences, how I portray them, and the level of detail that I use to talk about their experiences. It is of the utmost importance to me to keep my informants safe. Having experienced doxing during GamerGate, and having friends who have been stalked, assaulted, and threatened during that period, too, I will always tend towards being overprotective of my informants' identities, especially given that they are sharing their stories with me knowing that retribution is a possible consequence of speaking up. This is why only six voices are explicated in depth; like I said previously, all 52 people who I have been lucky enough to speak with and embed with are carried in this work in how I formed these ideas and how I am speaking about multiplicative precarit*ies*.

The informants that I want to highlight here are six current videogame production workers. Each of them have worked at least one full contract term in North American videogame production. Their jobs are all mostly coding and development-based labor except for one informant who performs quality assurance labor and community management labor in addition to coding labor. To restate: the informants whose experiences I am highlighting here have all seen how I have written about them and their experiences and have given me feedback to further clarify their interactions, feelings, and experiences. They are all also comfortable with me using their preferred pronouns. Aliases chosen by each informant are used in place of their real name. I will provide a brief summary of the key points of each interview that I am using for this chapter.

Mark (he/him): Mark has worked in videogame production since the late 80s. He has worked on big-budget triple-A titles that are still around today. During his time working on the aforementioned titles, he started as a programmer and was promoted to a senior management position when the company he worked for began to corporatize and do away with the flattened hierarchy he and his friends had started with. Mark now owns his own game company which has less than 10 people. He characterizes the places that he has worked at as hectic, passionate, and willing to put in long hours to produce good products. He characterizes his own studio as somewhere where everyone knows and has worked with each other for many years, so everyone is very chill and very in sync with one another. Mark resides in California.

Mark and I talked about his experiences coming up through videogame production. Where he started role-wise, the games that sparked passion in him, the game that ultimately led him to *become* a videogame production worker. We also talked about crunch, and his experiences with crunch. For him, crunch started as a challenge: it was a way of showing just *how* passionate he was about making a good product and the lengths that he would go to to prove that he was committed to videogame production. He acknowledges that this is not healthy in the long run, and contributed a great deal to burn out that he faced before opening his own company and doing consulting work.

Maria (she/they): Maria has worked in videogame production for five years; one of those years was as a contractor, and the other 4 have been as a full-time developer. She is a developer who specializes in weather systems and game physics. She have worked at the same company for all five of those years; the company is a medium-sized studio that produces mostly indie games. Maria characterized her workplace as fairly hands off until the need arises to become hands on, meaning that, as a studio, there are issues with time management amongst coworkers that have been addressed in the past. Other than an occasional intervention from management, Maria says that they enjoy working there most of the time. She resides in California.

Maria and I discussed at length questions around unionization. Who is it for? What does it do? Why are people pushing for it? Maria was very well informed about unionization efforts in videogame production and provided me with a lot to think about regarding how I talk about videogame production. Additionally, Maria brought up the possible issue of misattribution in how I talked about precarity and how/what I asked her and others about precarity. She said that precarity is not just "one thing," but rather, it is a whirlwind of things happening at once, growing, shrinking, leaving, and coming. She also talked to me about crunch and how destructive it is, yet how necessary it is due to how videogame production operates and the cultural ticks that consti-tute *why* videogame production needs crunch to operate.

Lauren (she/her): Lauren worked as a videogame production worker (developer) for four years and as a labor organizer/unionization organizer for two. She put in extreme hours to make herself available and open to helping others in videogame production understand the need for and benefits of col-lective action. She still works in videogame production at a medium-sized triple-A company. Lauren did not spend time characterizing her workplace, but instead, her work processes. She described those spaces and times as hectic, somewhat intimidating, and always challenging. On the labor organiz-ing side of things, Lauren characterized that as emotionally and physically draining, but ultimately the most rewarding thing she has ever done. Lauren resides in Massachusetts.

Lauren and I talked at length about crunch. She characterized crunch as the issue that got her into organizing in the first place. She doesn't like to see peo-ple suffer, therefore she started to try and find ways of alleviating the stress and precarity that she saw coworkers embroiled in. She also talked about how she served on a board for an initiative at one company she worked for. This board had a cross-section of people from across the company including QA workers, the CIO and CTO, marketing and communication workers, develop-ers, and even administrative workers. She characterized her time working on this board as odd at times, upsetting at other times, and downright frustrating most of the rest of the time. Lauren's peers in other departments could communicate with her, be nice, and share ideas, but anyone above their seniority in the company that was on this board was rude, derisive, and seemed to be speaking another language when talking about the games that were being made. Lauren characterized management as out of touch and completely obsessed with numbers rather than with people.

Coral (they/them): Coral has worked in videogame production for 10 contract cycles now. They have only worked as a developer, though they have worked on games, game engines, and game tools through their work. All of their contracts have been for very popular triple-A games. They have characterized their previous workplaces as mostly chill, but with the occasional transphobe which makes their job hard. They are currently in a contract with a triple-A company in California.

Coral and I ran the gamut of questions. We talked about everything from fandoms to queer modding and resistances in making games, to being trans and working in games, to struggling to date while working in games. They characterized their experience in videogame production both as a labor process and as a social experiment. They talked often about how the entanglements of videogame production like overwork, burnout, and obsession interrupted and rearranged their social life to the point where dating was next to impossible because their partners never shared the same level of passion for games that they did. Coral helped me to build upon what Maria brought up about misattribution. Coral and I had a long talk about what *is* precarious and precarity *means* (the same type of conversation you would hear in a 100-level Philosophy class) and how we can talk about it as such a multifaceted "thing."

Tara (she/her): Tara owns her own game studio in Canada. She characterized the studio as "indie" and said that it puts out games that evoke "indie aesthetics": pixelated graphics, 2D or isometric views, unique art styles. Tara has worked in videogame production for eight years and has worked at a few major triple-A companies. She decided that she wanted to change the work culture of videogame production and started her own company. She characterized her workplace as work-focused; they have largely dispensed with the "work while you play" ethic of triple-A production in favor of workers leaving the work they do *at* work instead of taking it home with them. She characterizes her workers as people who enjoy playing and making games, but equally enjoy having lives outside of making games. Tara resides in Canada.

Tara and I talked mostly about workplace culture. Having worked in a few triple-A, big-budget studios, her take on what workplace culture constituted was more than just who you see on a daily basis. It became about office politics; not tipping your hand too soon before you knew someone. There always seemed to be a sense of secrecy and possible backstabbiness at work in those environments. That's why, when Tara opened her own studio she were adamant about making it a place of work, not a typical "videogame production studio." She encourages a 40-hour work week with rare instances of possibly 45–50. She foreground the importance of understanding timelines, sticking to timelines, and communicating if something cannot get done in the time frame it was originally needed. Since her studio is fairly small still in personnel numbers, issues with communication are nonexistent for the most part; everyone gets on well, everyone is down to help everyone else if they need it, and everyone enjoyed the company of their coworkers and being able to work somewhere that values their time as much as it values their labor.

Malique (he/they): Malique is part-owner of a mobile-games company and has supported a very popular mobile title in addition to helping create another title that will release later this year. Though he does not self-identify as a "videogame developer," he does acknowledge that he carries out some of the labor associated with development. He also carries out labor associated with quality assurance and community management. He has worked here for four years, and he characterizes the company as "indie with a twist" meaning that workers are largely left alone to do their work, but they are aware that the company does have investors and bottom lines to meet. Malique resides in Texas.

Malique and I talked a lot about videogame production from a social aspect. Having shared roots in Austin, it was easy to talk about what bars we go to, who we would see, what barcades are better than others, so on and so forth. Malique also talked to me about sets of interactions with coworkers which presented quite an interesting case in collective action, but *not* unionization. Though he is adamant that this company does not have a union structure, Malique and his coworkers are so supportive of each other that, in effect, they have a class solidarity system where no one faces scrutiny alone and everyone shares the burden of work.

Theory into Praxis: The Case for Understanding Granular, Lived Experience

My informants helped me to understand that without further interrogation of what I meant when I was ascribing their stories and situations as "precarious," or said that they were facing "precarity," I was not doing enough to highlight and to substantiate what was happening in their lives and what these experiences actually meant. This is why it is necessary to take into account my informants' stories about their experiences working in videogame production to talk about the intersections and entanglements that form precarity as they understand and experience it. For my informants, the term "precarity" is not just an adjective or an attribution. It is a noun: they deal with precarity. Precarity is sometimes a force in their lives just the same as a glass wall is.

It is an adverb: a situation becomes precarious. Precarity does not manifest and stay still; it shifts, grows, and changes. It is an affect: they feel precarious, or they feel *precariousness*. My informants feel precarious in that they are unsure of their next step or next job, and they feel precariousness in the arrangement of set actions and workflow of the job that they are completing. Again, precarity is not a static thing; precarity encompasses actions and bodily attributions, facilitates decision-making, and exists as a manifested obstacle in the lives of my informants.

This move from the singular "precarity" to the multiple "precarities" is not meant to signal an expansion of what circumstances could be conceived of to *create* precarity. Instead, the move to multiple precarities is meant to signal that there are mitigating factors and attributions that happen on a personal, human level that are complicit in creating the circumstances in which precarity can present. It does no good to continue trying to lay bare what named, specific actions that happen in labor conditions are "precarious." Crunch, overwork, toxic workplace conditions, operationalization of passion, the capitalist socius' deathdrive towards overcoding bodies into being purely productive bodies etc. are forms of precarity. The literature that this book has reviewed and relied on to come up with frameworks show that, in line with Walsh, Han, and Moore's individual contributions in regard to what is and is not precarious, those activities are theoretically backed as "precarious." Therefore, I have no interest in further defining what *events* are precarious. Instead, I am interested in picking at the underlying causes for why those events can be considered precarious to some people and not others, to differing degrees, with differing attachments, contestations, and understandings of why or how those things are precarious.

Using my informants' stories about their time and experience working in videogame production as evidence, this chapter draws conclusions about three general themes that are present within my informants' stories that provide more context for the gray spaces in between theoretical distinctions of what "precarity" is. Those themes are: trauma, vulnerability, and risk. These three sets of themes, while separate, are highly intertwined and reflect how insidious the concept of "precarity" is and how multifaceted its appearances are. This is the reason why it is imperative to dig down into the themes from the previous two chapters to better understand just what issues are at stake when making a move towards multiple, multifaceted *precarities*. Returning to my introduction where I used work from Paul Walsh, Clara Han, and Phoebe Moore to help triangulate what a definition of "precarity" could be, my move towards "precarit*ies*" does not preclude or excise their work. Through these three pieces of definitional work in other fields, the idea of what *facilitates* precarity becomes easier to talk about, but the act of pinpointing what precarity *is* is still out of reach by relying on these works alone. We can ascertain that precarity has roots in, and is exacerbated by, neoliberalism, casualization of labor, and the strip-mining of worker protections and worker welfare. But the extenuating circumstances of the people involved in the everyday systemic labor of late-stage, neoliberal capitalism are unaccounted for, which is where the move towards multiplicative precarit*ies* becomes useful.

Trauma

During my time talking to my informants, trauma often came connected to what they deemed as negative or "precarious." Trauma, in common parlance, refers to a deeply distressing or disturbing experience. Of these six people whose stories I am sharing, nearly all of them talked about trauma at some point in their careers. How they each approached or validated their own experiences, though, shifted drastically from person to person. 47 of the 52 videogame production workers I have embedded with and been able to talk about their stories reported feeling trauma as well. Within those 47, some talked about self-inflicted trauma in the form of overwork: the overwork that they were expected to perform should be worn as a badge of honor—you're doing a cool job, millions of people are going to play your work, and you have to work your way through the negative stuff if you want to make your own game some day. Other informants talked about issues of sexual harassment and discrimination. Since videogame production has been and continues to be largely male dominated,[1] the perpetuation of hypermasculinity and the necessity of dominance within videogame production spaces creates an environment, as D'Anastasio says of Riot Games, ultimately built for a male gaze and only concerned with male advancement: both of people into positions of leadership, and of male-coded ideology. Still others talked about power abuse from superiors at their companies. For each of my informants, they experienced things in their time in videogame production that fundamentally shifted how they approached production, how they viewed their own entanglement in production, or somehow tainted their initial conception of the role that being passionate about games played in being successful.

I want to highlight three examples of trauma that my informants brought up as a way to contextualize how "trauma" as a concept is not static, and depends on circumstances beyond a generalizable theoretical framework to determine *why* and *what* is traumatic about a series of events. The experiences I will be talking about in this section are from Mark, Lauren, and Coral. When talking about "trauma" in regard to my informants, it's important to remember that they have vastly different quantifications of what trauma is and what it means. In recent informal conversations with Coral, I talked to them about the idea that trauma might be an underlying cause of precarity, and a reason why referring to situations that I'd talked with them about as a catch-call "precarity" wasn't correct, and thus necessitates a move towards multiple *precarities*. I asked them what they thought of trauma when thinking about their time in videogames, and they raised a very important point:

> I feel like I have the most fucked up sense of trauma. Like, someone could yell at me and I could casually drop that that traumatized me, but, like I have told you, I just fucking truck away at work, get transphobia'd, and still keep going. Where does the line get drawn, man? I don't even know what traumatizes me or could traumatize me anymore.

Similarly, Mark talked about trauma as something that's not neat or clearly understandable in a conversation we had recently.

> I uh, I remember talking about o-or well, mentioning trauma the last time we spoke, actually. It made me think about if I was using that term too loosely. And you know, I-I don't think I was. What happened was a breaking point. Something that uh . . . I couldn't necessarily come back from. But then, I also have these fond memories of overworking prior to that. Did I ruin it b-because of my dad? Or was it just finally my time to stop wanting to do it? I don't know. And I think that it would be drastically different if it hadn't been at that point in my life.

Again, similarly, Lauren talked about how traumatic experiences don't necessarily create a recognizable or quantifiable event immediately; it's the fallout of that event or events that define the type of, level of, reaction to, and understanding of what elements were traumatic.

> Do I remember how it felt when that jackass said that stuff about me and my team? Yes. But, somehow, that doesn't feel traumatic. I have heard people say similar things before but it hasn't been directed at me. No, it was when I was talking to people, and trying to contextualize how or . . . or I guess why that happened that it became real. When coworkers who I had just met at [COMPANY] started talking about similar past experiences and saying it with just such resignation, that's when the stuff that happened felt real. More weighty.

Mark, Coral, and Lauren's events and experiences with trauma share similar characteristics: power abuse, misattribution, workplace culture, crunch, and collective action. But what is important is the granularity of the experiences that each informant has shared. Nothing about their experiences is the same; none of it is quantifiable. Using this definitional work, nothing about their experiences lends itself to saying "this and this are aspects of trauma that are directly related to precarity." Instead, their experiences provide framing for saying "trauma is a personal affect, and these informants shared with me these aspects of their experiences that they considered traumatic."

Mark spoke at length in previous conversations about his attachment to crunch; he recognized that, when he entered videogame production, overwork had not yet coalesced as a way of conceptualizing the work that they were doing. It was simply "work," and he and his team committed themselves to that work because they were passionate about videogames. Mark, towards the end of this time at their first studio, was burnt out on overwork because of the corporatization of the company. The initial allure of videogame production as a rogue, lawless endeavor was lost when the organization established hierarchies and unflattened. The last session of crunch that Mark worked was where he located the source of trauma that we spoke about during our conversations.

My father passed around 3 months before crunch started on [GAME]. I thought "You know, this will take my mind off things, and give me some distance." Well, it did not. The entire time that we were crunching, I had my boss and his boss breathing down my neck. A-and usually, that wouldn't bother me. But there was something so oppressive about it. I remember very vividly the set of events that led up to me feeling . . . I . . . traumatized. I guess. By it. [. . .] We went into Tom's [NOTE: Tom is the alias given to Mark's boss in this story] office and he just pushed a report at me and looked at me like I was a-an invalid or something. All he asked was "So, when are you going to get this stuff done that should have been done three weeks ago?" I don't know what happened. The past month and a half just flooded back in on me and I realized that regardless of what I was doing at work, it was like I was undoing the work that other people were doing. I wasn't, but it felt like it in my mind. A-and the way that Tom asked me this . . . I had a nervous breakdown right there. So much stuff piled up on top of other stuff on top of other stuff that I finally broke. Whereas I had always been killer-efficient, on top of my game, all of a sudden, I realized that I didn't belong in this system anymore. My way of doing things wasn't the way of the world anymore. I realized that crunch, and overwork, had, for me, been a way of pushing things uh . . . pushing things out of my head. So I didn't have to deal with them. [. . .] I started my own thing so that I could make *sure* that I worked with people who respected my values and thought the same way that I did. I never wanted to be the cause of someone else hurting like I did. It fundamentally changed my value system and the value system that I predicated my work on. [. . .] If I think about it from someone else's perspective like my wife's, it's clear that crunch wasn't something that I ever should have uh . . . c-confided in or valorized. It wasn't and isn't the key to success. It was just mini traumas over and over again. I-it just was a more attractive and more productive uh . . . uh, way to push through things that I didn't want to deal with.

This was a shocking turn of events in my experience with Mark. In previous conversations we'd had, crunch had been something that he was proud of, and that he talked about past experiences with fondly. Mark, at this point, had approximately eight years' worth of time invested in videogame production.

He was used to hard work; to overwork. He reveled in it, and he used it as a way of characterizing his commitment to videogames. In doing so, crunch became a cruelly optimistic attachment. Instead of that attachment being predicated on advancing forward into a better life monetarily, or eschewing precarity that was labor-based, this attachment was a regression away from issues outside of the realm of videogame production. In allowing for crunch to occupy this space for him and allowing crunch to become attached to him both as a sense of prideful duty and as a way of escaping difficult issues in life, the circumstances surrounding crunch for Mark became what he feared most: the *reason* that he would have to regress and deal with issues that he had been eschewing.

Lauren located trauma not in a set of events that transpired, but in how she *unpacked* those events and what those events implied to her and about her regarding the nature of videogame production. Lauren served on a cross-sectional board at her studio that was meant to represent all levels of employees and was meant to be an open forum to discuss progress, questions, and concerns. Lauren experienced blatant power abuse when speaking at this cross-sectional meeting one day:

> Anyway, we were talking, and this person interrupts me to say "your team needs to hurry the fuck up because it seems like a pretty mindless task that you're working on." Then he said "we should just pay some monkeys to do it," referring to Indian people. I think everyone who had half a conscience was so shocked by that that we all just froze. I remember making eye-contact with someone in marketing, and their eyes being about as large as a saucer. Then, I just got up and left. I couldn't believe what I had heard.

In the wake of that event, it became apparent that this was more than just a one-off event; as Lauren spoke with other members of different teams across the studio, she soon came to realize that not only had other workers experienced similar interactions at this studio, but at other studios they had worked at as well. Though not as blatantly racist, nor necessarily as blatantly abusive, Lauren characterized, others had similar experiences. In the following weeks, as she unpacked what had happened to her, what her peers had told her about their experiences, and what those implications meant, she realized how deeply disturbing those implications were.

> After all of that, I just kind of spun out. I'm an empath. I don't like to hear about people suffering. And for people that I highly respect to report similar stuff had happened to them here and other places? I went into overdrive. Unionization and collective action became the single most important thing to me, like a mania. I mean, I knew that this stuff happened, you know, but it didn't click with me until the few weeks after this. It shook me to my core. What were we

doing here? Why is this kind of stuff just an expectation? It hit me that passion might pay the bills, but trauma isn't, or, well, shouldn't, be an expectation too.

The initial event that Lauren experienced could have been where trauma was demarked for her. Instead, it was the implications of that event that became traumatic and catalyzed her to further pursue means of helping her coworkers and peers start the process of unionizing and creating cohesive collective action plans. Lauren entered videogame production under the impression that all parts of the process functioned to serve the end-goal of bringing videogames to life. She acknowledged that there was roughness in the process, even before experiencing these events, hence her drive to unionize. But it was the distinction that the different parts of videogame production *weren't* all serving the same ends that changed her way of talking about, thinking about, and interacting with videogame production. She talked to me about her self-reported mania in the wake of these events and juxtaposed it with the come-down from that mania as being "the thing that really drove home how, pardon me, completely fucked videogame production was." Instead of allowing disillusionment and apathy to characterize the post-trauma landscape that Lauren found herself in, she talked about how, even though she were not able to maintain the mania that she experienced in those first few weeks, these events fundamentally reaffirmed that what she was doing was more important and more fulfilling to her than the act of producing videogames.

Coral paints their experience with videogame production as "fucking complicated." Though they have yet to obtain a full-time core development position and have only had contract work, they're still hopeful that they'll be able to break through and obtain a permanent position in the near future. They liken this duality to an abusive relationship, however:

> Man, fuckin', I know that I should just go do something else. I know it. At the end of the day, I just want to love what I do. I don't think I would love software production. [long pause] It's abusive, you know. I guess I'm abusing myself? I know that not being in videogame production, I would be happier in the long run. Or, at least less stressed, maybe even actually appreciated. But man, there's nothing appealing about it. At least in videogame production, I'm already here, I know how to roll with the punches and just . . . I dunno. Get by? Do my thing? Here, I feel necessary. There's excitement and passion. But there's also small borderline traumas every time I hear that I'm not getting a permanent job after it was dangled in front of my damn face. I always swear it's the last time. But I cool off for a week or two, go back to basics and play some stuff that I haven't played in a while and I fall in love with it all all over again. I don't really know what to do.

For Coral, videogame production has proven volatile: from job instability and false hope about being hired full-time to their experiences being actively discriminated against, they have experienced a lot of situations that could be considered precarious. But the situations in and of themselves are not what cause this informant to pause when considering their relationship with video-game production. It's the attachment to the feeling of falling out of love and then back in love with videogames that they self-reportedly go through at the end of nearly every contract cycle that bookends the complicated relationship they have with putting all of themselves into the act of production. In previous conversations, Coral detailed how they commit to work during a typical contract, and their time commitment is admirable. Though they have scaled back their commitment to work, they still report that with each contract, they do not give up the hope that they actually *will* be hired full-time at the end of that contract. That means that they continue to put themselves into each project and commit enough energy that it becomes a point of trauma when they learn that their efforts were in vain.

Using these informants' explicit experiences with trauma, and their understandings of what trauma *is*, it becomes possible to start to locate how trauma is an aspect of precarity. Much like precarity, trauma is a shifting presence in a person's life; what is traumatic for one is not necessarily traumatic for all. Additionally, finding something traumatic entails looking past just the spatiotemporal presence of the event or events themselves and instead looking at the web of attachments and intertwinements that reach into the past and the present where that person finds themselves co-located with what they find traumatic. Trauma is slippery as is precarity.

Vulnerability

Vulnerability is understood to be a state of being exposed to the possibility of mental or physical attack or harm. Being vulnerable or experiencing vulnerability can be talked about in multiple circumstances, and attached to multiple situations. Akin to trauma, vulnerability to my informants was not an easily quantifiable thing, nor did it mean the same thing across any conversation that I had with any informant. For some of the 51 informants that reported some sort of interaction or thought with vulnerability, vulnerability was a state of existence. They felt powerless to change the state of things around them, or they felt that they were, as Maria said "belly up, waiting for someone to attack." For others, vulnerability was a mindset that came after a set of events. Coral reported that, after each stint as a contract employee, they were worn down and burnt out and lacked the will to self-preserve; that "if someone literally asked me to jump off a fucking bridge, I'd do it." Malique characterized vulnerability not as something negative, but as a place of trust that only certain people had access to. Whereas during work hours, he was expected to keep a stalwart façade, after hours, his trusted friends and his partner gave him the space to be vulnerable—to cry, to complain, to cheer, to experience emotions that he could not, or did not feel comfortable, sharing with their employees.

Of all 52 people I have interviewed and embedded with throughout my academic career, Mark was the only one who did not talk explicitly about being or feeling vulnerable, of experiencing vulnerability. Akin to trauma, each person's conception of and colocation with vulnerability was wildly different. In this section, I want to highlight specifically the conversations I had with Maria and Malique. Maria and Malique presented ways of thinking about and experiencing vulnerability that challenge how we conceive of the common understanding of the concept. Both of these informants touched on aspects of the very basic definition of vulnerability, but expanded on what it *meant* to be exposed. Whereas the definition of vulnerability takes away the autonomy of those experiencing vulnerability, Maria and Malique acknowledged that they had control over being vulnerable—to some extent. Maria talked about vulnerability as being implicit in working in videogame production outside of a management position:

> You're always liable to be fired, I have learned that the hard way. Even if you are full-time, you can get fired for pretty much anything. I suppose that kind of vulnerability is sobering. I have been lucky that I haven't worked somewhere where people got fired for seemingly no reason, but I have worked places where getting fired has been threatened. It's tough. It is very tough to come to work and work on something that you know isn't working but being scared of taking initiative to change it because you're scared that you're going to be fired. It renders you belly up, waiting for someone to attack you or your ideas when it's just easier to resign yourself to the fact that what you are working on may not work but just doing it anyway. It's a job after all.

When asked about whether she had seen anyone take initiative and what happened, she recounted a story of a coworker at a previous company who, during production, was insistent that not using a workflow program like AGILE or Scrum was slowing down production. Maria said that at every opportunity, he brought up the boons of workflows and it finally got to the point where he got yelled at and threatened to be fired in front of the entire group if he brought the subject up again.

Malique similarly talked about feeling vulnerable, especially toward fans; part of him felt that the games that he produced at his company needed to be a certain way to appease fans and to continue generating revenue.

You have to listen to your fans. I started this company because I had the goal of making games that my friends and I would enjoy. Simple as that. But that was in 2016. Things have changed. The world has changed. Lately, it's caught me on my back foot as some of the things we have talked about have been panned by fans. It's hard to take that kind of critique when you're working on something that you, personally, want and are provisioning for. But, at the end of the day, we're a business and we have to give fans the experiences that will make them happy.

Malique, though, also spoke about vulnerability in another way: as a way of self-care.

I don't know if this is too much, but I value being vulnerable with my friends and boyfriend. I love them. I know they love me. I know that I can show emotions around them and that they aren't going to prey on me. They're going to support me when I need it, give me a shoulder to cry on when I need it, and cheer with me when I need it. It's all circle-of-trust stuff.

In this context, Malique provides an interesting interpretation of the scope of vulnerability: it might mean something negative in relation to some situations, but it is also a source of power; a source of radical self-care and trust-building that allows him to reclaim control over both the situations that are occurring in his life and the term "vulnerability" itself.

Malique and Maria provide important contextualization and a reminder that vulnerability (like trauma) is slippery. It is not static, it takes many forms, and it doesn't translate cleanly from situation to situation. But unlike trauma, the concept of vulnerability does not render the person experiencing vulnerability as scarred or fundamentally marked as "traumatized." Vulnerability more than anything is attributive and tends to exist in relation to other aspects of precarity. That existence is predicated on entanglements, affects, and events that form the temporal capacity for that moment to render someone vulnerable both in a positive and a negative way. Maria, throughout our conversations, has been very careful to clarify the terms that she uses, how she uses them, and what the impact of those terms has on what she is talking about. Talking about vulnerability was no exception. Maria talked about vulnerability in two ways: the first way is as a pall across her existence in videogame production. She was careful to quantify the *amount* of vulnerability she felt, though.

Like I said, working in games is just an invitation to always be vulnerable. There's no job that you can have that marks you as "safe." Look at Telltale. They made amazing games, but there was some kink in the system and they went belly up. Same for places like Lionhead and THQ and Insomniac, right?

You're never safe. Even if you make games that transcend the era they were made in, that doesn't matter. What I'm getting at is, in the moment, I don't think of myself as vulnerable. It is a meta commentary. I don't go throughout my day scared that someone is going to fire me. I would go insane! It's background noise, but it is ever-present background noise. It's like tinnitus. It doesn't mean much on its own. Just a buzzing. But in context, it means *a lot*. But we don't think "in context." Or, at least, I don't. I take things moment to moment, hour to hour, day to day.

Maria's quantification of vulnerability, and the way that she contextualize how she feels it, or rather, doesn't feel it is telling regarding how we can think about living with vulnerability. The precarious element of possibly not having a job if a project does not make money is not native or unique to videogame production. Late-stage capitalism and neoliberalism have created labor regimes that have become casualized and contingent. We live with the "background noise" of knowing that, should some catastrophe occur that renders the institution we work for nonproductive or incapable of recouping a loss, we will lose our ability to make money. And under subjectivation from the capitalist socius, we are somewhat acutely aware that we are productively shaped working bodies that are able to find similar work in similar institutions. To Maria, though, this is not an ever-present or looming threat—it does render her perpetually vulnerable. Instead, it is an element of the job that she is aware of: she is aware that by the nature of capitalism and the videogame production industry, she is vulnerable to tumult. She also realizes that this space of mind is not the same for everyone.

But that's just how I live. I know people and I work with people who are scared to lose their jobs. For some reason or another, some of my friends live and work like if they don't commit to the job or they don't do their absolute best, they will lose that job. I don't want to say they live in fear, but they are fearful of this aspect of the industry. And I think that it is something that employers can take advantage of. For me, I like working in games, but I know that I have other options. I have worked in other industries. I mean, working in any industry is a risk, if we want to get really meta about it, right? But I don't let that fear drive me.

For Maria, vulnerability coexisted with fear in the context of losing a job. She observed this with coworkers and friends. The fear of losing a job is the inverse side of the type of work commitment that Coral had outlined in previous conversations where they commit as hard as they can to a project and put all of themselves into it, even though they have scaled back this practice over consecutive contracts. Instead of working hard to obtain a job like Coral says that they do, Maria has characterized people she knows as working to *keep* a job; She recognizes that the aspect of vulnerability that she characterized as background noise for herself is not necessarily that minor for others.

Akin to Maria, Malique characterized the videogame production industry as creating an environment where everyone is vulnerable to being fired for nothing. Malique talked about instances when he still worked for a company that he did not own when his peers were fired midproject for things that were not apparent.

> When I still worked at my previous company, the ship was run tight. We were expected to fall in line and do our work, be productive, and don't ruffle feathers. For some people, that didn't sit right. [. . .] I had a coworker who constantly worked late. She was there when I got there in the morning, and stayed past when I left. For all intents and purposes, I thought she was the most productive one in our group. One day, she got fired pretty unceremoniously. Taken into the office, given an excuse about downsizing, let go. It was baffling. Even now, I can't figure out what it was. Having some years between then and now, I almost wonder if it was a veiled threat to the rest of us. She was a workhorse. What other reason would you have to fire someone like that unless you wanted to send a message? [. . .] I know that we're not exactly "corporate" here, but I still have to sometimes mindgame employees. But man, never like that. I could be wrong, though, of course. It's just the only thing that I can think of that. Even if Piotra[2] had a bad attitude, constantly complained, or constantly was knocking on our bosses door to tattle or something, the amount of work she put in was just . . . too valuable. It must have been a threat. I can't think of any other reason.

This instance stuck with Malique, and he characterized it as something ominous. In retrospect, and given the context of his current job where he co-owns a studio, he couldn't think of any other reason but it being some sort of veiled threat, or play for their team to increase productivity, which they did.

> In the wake of that, yeah, we were all firing on all cylinders. Now we had to pick up the slack of Piotra, which for all accounts, was the work of two people, and we had to basically jump someone new in when they hired them. Our hands were forced, and we were basically precrunch crunching just to show that we wanted to be there.

In this instance, the vulnerable nature of working in videogame production existed alongside control. Malique provides a way to think about institutional mechanisms such as hiring and firing as not only effecting the person being hired or fired, but as a way of ensuring continuity in the subjectivation that the production space favors. Malique admittedly did not have access to the extenuating circumstances around this employee's firing, but he did have a special context from which to examine this incident. He admits that part of running a studio (which I would expand to "running a business in general") is mindgaming employees. He briefly contextualized "mindgaming" as: "not abusing employees or gaslighting them, but sometimes they have ideas that you know will sink your company and you have to kind of . . . nudge them towards your way of thinking by helping them understand how damaging their idea could be to the fans' experience."

Malique presents an alternative to just collocating vulnerability with systems in capitalism. Instead, he talks about the act of being vulnerable and choosing who to be vulnerable with as a radical form of self-care and healing.

> When I think of being vulnerable, or feeling vulnerable, I can't help but think about how that characterizes my closest relationships. It's still related to videogames, of course, but it isn't ABOUT videogames. I make myself vulnerable with my boyfriend and my close friends. They get to see the parts of me that no one else does. When I'm sad, when I'm happy, frustrated, mad, burnt out. These are the people I rely on to accept me as I am and allow me a space to feel these feelings. It isn't about being in this state for extended periods of time. It's just contextual. Like, if Tim, my partner, is having a bad day, I want him to be able to feel like he can open up to me and know that I'll support him however I can.

Malique was able to locate vulnerability not in relation to precarity, but in relation to healing. Malique coopted what, for most of my informants, is a negative attribution due to the line of work that he is in, or due to power imbalances within his jobs, and flip the script. Instead of being concerned with the negative situations and characterizations that vulnerability contains, Malique talks about its healing power. But, its healing power is located in relation to *trust*. The circumstances where this informant was able to use vulnerability as a positive force coalesce around trusted friends and their partner; their "circle-of-trust."

Vulnerability can be located in relation to precarity in a number of circumstances and in a number of varying degrees of severity. But it can also be located alongside self-care, forging trusting bonds with peers in similar situations, and can act as a moment of respite in an otherwise tumultuous environ. The act of *being vulnerable* is multifaceted and depends on the immediate situation that a person finds themselves in, the suite of entanglements and attachments that that person brings to the situation, and the mitigating factors of what type of situation they find themselves in: is the context for vulnerability a social situation? A labor situation? An interpersonal situation? The context where we find ourselves in a position of vulnerability is as important as the events themselves. Akin to trauma, what we conceptualize as vulnerability swings widely depending on a suite of factors.

Risk and (Re)distribution

When talking to my informants, the subject of risk came up in a multitude of different contexts. Risk, for some informants, complimented a state of vulnerability: they risk working in a job that makes them vulnerable, they risk creating a hostile work environment should their work be subpar, they risk their physical and mental health by committing to crunch. Some informants located risk not as a state of being but as a thing to be shared. At work, risk can be shared across an entire time. Coral talked about "doing risky things with code" that could have cost their team time and resources if the risk didn't pay off. Malique talked about risk redistribution in the same way that he talked about vulnerability with his partner. Between jobs, Malique's partner had to support them both while Malique tried to secure a new job. This led to him cofounding own company, which then presented different aspects of redistributed risk in that Malique's partner had to support both of them while the company sought funding.

Risk is understood to be a situation where someone is exposed to some element of danger, uncertainty, or potential loss. In a similar way to vulnerability, risk exists alongside other elements of precarity. For something to be "of risk" or "risky," it has to present elements that are unstable or uncertain, but must also present elements that are possibly lucrative. Unlike vulnerability or trauma, risk can expand and retract to encompass multiple people, situations, and entanglements. As with Malique, one person can enter a risky situation, and then that risk can be redistributed across other people to help shoulder the potentially destructive element of the risk if what is being sought doesn't pay dividends. In this section, I want to highlight conversations with Coral, Tara, and Malique. All six informants acknowledged that they have engaged in what they perceive to be risky behavior or been in situations that presented risk. Similarly, 48 out of 52 informants identified that they had been in risky or risk-adjacent situations. But these three informants presented nuanced and multifaceted understandings of where risk lived in their lives, how risk has led to trauma and vulnerability, and how risk becomes an agent of change for better or worse.

Tara, during our first conversation back in 2017, talked about the act of committing to videogame production against her parents' wishes as risky not just in that she had heard how tumultuous the job market could be, but also that she risked alienating and straining already strained relations with her parents.

I hid that I was focusing on videogame production while doing my software engineering degree! I didn't tell anyone for the longest time. Finally, it got to be too much and on Christmas break of my junior year, I told my mom when my dad had gone out to do something. She said that she would support me, but that she didn't think I was doing the right thing. As she said "Videogames aren't serious. They're frivolity and your father doesn't like them."

Tara's family has a history of being in software production. Both her parents have worked in software production for Fortune 100 companies, her siblings have their own consulting business, and it was expected that Tara would follow an equally "serious" trajectory in software production. Tara acknowledged that, given the prevalence of software engineers in her family, that she was at least acquainted with the employment risks of going into videogame production, but this did not deter her because "I don't just want to be another cog making an OS [operating system] or some bloatware. I want to make something people like." The risk that her job path posed to the relationship with her family was something that she did consider heavily, and it proved to be somewhat founded.

> I didn't tell my dad until I graduated. And he saw it in the freaking commencement material! Where I graduated, we did general commencement and then our own department commencement, so he didn't see it until then. He didn't talk to me for a week after he found out. *laughs* I mean, we're fine now, but he still worries a lot about me, and he does that typical Indian thing where he compares me to brothers. "Oh Samuel³ makes $200,000 a year. You could be doing that too!" I don't care dad! *laughs* But I mean, there's a reason why I stayed in Vancouver after I graduated. They live up north. I don't have to see them every day. My dad means well, but it's a lot to hear that kind of stuff um . . . a-all the time. You know?

One of the factors of risk for Tara does not have roots in labor or economic concerns, but instead in familial and emotional concerns. Her family had clear expectations that Tara "just didn't live up to"; she traded economic prosperity for doing something that she enjoyed. Tara chalked her father's badgering up largely to cultural expectation: she did not follow her father's wishes *and* she pursued something that her family considered unbefitting of the time, effort, and money invested in her college experience. For this informant though, the potential job risks and state of vulnerability that their family attributed to videogame production did not outweigh their need to do something interesting and that they would enjoy doing. They spoke about their experience in videogame production as largely positive, and their family's worries unfounded.

> I know that people have a bad time in videogames, but I think I got really lucky working for [COMPANY]. I also think that it might have to do with being a [PLATFORM] company, too. There's more iteration, less "you must finish this

and ship it now!" We get to work on bug fixes, content, and other stuff and roll it out as it gets done, not by a deadline. So I think for me, the risk hasn't really been there in the same way as it is for other people.

Though they acknowledge that they are lucky to be working where they are and in the platform that they do, they also acknowledge that their experiences are somewhat nontypical. But even within a nontypical situations that Lauren characterized as largely positive, risk is still like a background noise, to borrow from Maria.

For Malique, risk manifested in two discrete ways. The first way was when he talked about opening his own studio following getting burnt out of working for someone else. He understood that, even though they had novel ideas about how to run a studio, how to treat workers, and how to get work done, that that did not guarantee success by any means. He also recognized the risk of finding investors or seed money because of the underlying expectations that the partners would have about making a return on investment. The second manifestation of risk in Malique's life links back to what he said about vulnerability; instead of shouldering the entirety of the financial burden that starting up a company would put on him, the risk was shared with their significant other. Akin to well-known stories of spouses supporting game creators like Eric Barone of Stardew Valley fame, Malique characterized a similar experience of his partner allowing them to redistribute the financial, emotional, and temporal risk of opening a studio by supporting both of them during the startup period and assisting him in finding potential investors that would be more understanding of his vision:

> Tim helped me every step of the way. Not only was he there for me when I was burning out, he gave me space when I needed it, cooked me dinner and made sure I was ok when I was so depressed I couldn't move, and so much more. Then, when I started talking about opening my own studio, Tim supported me from the beginning. He knew what I wanted to do, and he believed that I could do. I told him that I was scared I wouldn't be able to live and that I'd drain my savings, and that's when he suggested we move in together. *laughs* It didn't stop there, though. As I was getting everything together, he was sending me referrals to venture capital companies he worked with! Like, daily. Tim was always there and he helped me shoulder a lot of this burden.

Malique was able to locate risk not *just* as a state of being exposed to potentially damaging circumstances with no fallback, but also as something to be redistributed across support networks. His partner's financial, emotional, and business support allowed for Malique to offload some of the risk that he was facing by opening his own studio. In doing so, the precarities that can manifest in this branch of videogame production were almost entirely mitigated. As a note, this is a special case of risk distribution in videogame production. Malique's ability to start and maintain his own studio, and to make that studio successful, eschews the need to reckon with certain forms of precarity like instability, negative workplace culture, and opaque meritocracy.

Coral, however, provides what I would consider a stereotypical case of risk distribution. In much the same way that Malique relied on his partner to help him shoulder some of the burden of switching jobs and creating a studio, Coral relied on their sibling Bethany (alias provided by Coral) to provide them with the same emotional support, and at points, financial support.

> Me and Bethany both moved out to Los Angeles because we wanted to shake things up. Midwest sucks, the people there suck, so we said no and left. Anyway, Bethany is a marketing genius, so she got a job like . . . 5 seconds after we landed making a hundred billion dollars a year. For me, things rolled a little slower. Shit took me like three months to get anything. The first contract gig I landed was out in Riverside, which is like 30 miles from where we were living. [. . .] Since things were kinda fucky getting going, I had to ask Bethany to basically sugar-sibling me for like . . . gas and stuff for about a month and a half until I got paid and started selling plasma.

For Coral to begin to be successful in videogame production, they had to rely on their sibling to help them with transport, food, shelter, and other necessities until they could get established. Coral talked about the slowness of getting a job in videogame production as being unexpected; their sibling got a job almost immediately making six figures while it took them almost three months to obtain a contract position. They also talked about the initial move as

> kind of a boner on my part. I didn't think it'd take so fucking long to get a job. Like, I'm trans, just give me a job now please. *laughs* I don't guess I realized it was gonna be that risky to just up and move without a plan. Who'd have thought.

Though Coral retrospectively acknowledges that there was risk inherent in the plan of moving cross-country without having a job offer in hand, they were able to mitigate the worst effects due to the distribution of risk across themselves and their sibling. Having that support from their sibling was integral for them to be able to find a job that suited them and that they would be happy in, even if it was just a temporary job. This informant talked about how their sibling was their emotional "rock" during the process of trying to find a full-time core developer role.

Bethany listened to me bitch soooo much and so long. Like, I constantly complained how I couldn't find anything except contract work. Now, I lived with her for 2 ½ years before I finally had enough saved to strike out on my own. And during that time, I worked three contract gigs. Two of those dangled the old wormy of "if you work hard enough, we might have a job open up" in front of me. Bethany was my rock the whole time, though. I'd work until like 10, 11 at night, come home, and she'd have me like . . . a fuckin' bento box ready to eat every night. It was insane. She also helped me think through next steps, alternatives, everything that I needed when I was about to have a goddamn breakdown.

Coral's experiences with risk distribution present what I think is a more typical case of risk *redistribution*, but not of risk itself. They are aware of the vulnerabilities of being contract and not getting lucky getting hired on at the end of books. They were able to mitigate the worst of the possible emotional and psychical traumas by having their sibling to talk them through problems, help them problem-solve, provide them with emotional and financial security, and to make sure that they ate healthy food when they were exhausted.

Using these informants' experiences with risk, it becomes possible to locate where risk intersects with precarity. Risk is not a prolonged situational aspect of precarity like vulnerability is. Risk, instead, *is* a static state. It still depends on the person who is experiencing or contemplating potentially risky circumstances as to the level of risk involved and what that risk means for them, but a set of events either is or is not risky. Whereas a person can *be* vulnerable or experience vulnerability, someone cannot experience risk as a prolonged state unless they are repeating risky actions or behavior with enough regularity to constantly be in a state of risk (the easiest example of this type of behavior might be gambling). The set of events at hand have the demarcation of some variation of "is risky": is risky, isn't that risky, is very risky, etc. Risk can, however, be a mediating factor in other aspects of precarity. Undertaking a set of risky decisions can prolong or induce vulnerability, it can traumatize, it can produce other unaccountable attachments and entanglements that, if the risk was not taken, would not otherwise exist.

Precarities

This chapter is concerned with making formative steps towards a theorization of "precarity" as multifaceted and multiplicative: precari*ties*. As I stated previously, "precarity" as an umbrella term is useful to do a lot of heavy theoretical lifting that does not directly point to specific characteristics of, instances of, or entanglements with the underlying elements of precarity. However, this book's entanglement with cruel optimism and the capitalist socius' need for subjectivatable bodies begs for closer inspection of precarity.

Precarity, as this chapter proves, is not a static or singular thing. On its own, it can function as a way of talking about a situation or person, but it can also accompany and compliment the concepts that I discussed in the previous chapter. Precarity can be a paired attribution to a person who is experiencing vulnerability or trauma. A precarious situation can also be a traumatic or risky situation. Precarity shifts and changes to suit circumstances and labor conditions. It morphs to encompass and exacerbate personal attachments to objects, people, or concepts. It spills out from singular events, encompasses fallout and preceding circumstances of events. Precarity is an interchangeable term that encompasses the things that this chapter outlines and more and it is also its own conceptualization of potentially negative circumstances. The distillation of precarity to these three terms is a first step towards a better and more thoroughly theorization of the multifaceted nature *of* precarity, but these terms only encompass a small, observable part of precarity specifically for six workers in videogame production that all come from similar working conditions but have experiences, affects, and dispositions that render them individual and one of a kind and unquantifiable.

The concepts that this chapter covers open up consideration for what the concept of "precarity" means, what we conceive of as "precarious," and how we engage with, attribute, and think about "being precarious." Trauma, vulnerability, and risk can all be located alongside and within precarity. Using my informants' stories, I was able to observe some generalizable phenomenon and circumstance that can be collocated with precarity, with one another, with and embedded in cruel optimism, and contoured and contained by the capitalist socius. Inductive observations are helpful for establishing generalizable concepts; my informants' stories are no different. But I want to couch what is generalizable about their experience and what is not. Just because all or most of my informants experienced trauma, vulnerability, or risk does not mean that these concepts transfer cleanly to other workers in videogame production. What is beyond the scope of this book is exploring the wild web of entanglements that go into characterizing just one person's affects, attachments, predispositions, cognitive processes, and psychical energy. Therefore, it would be irresponsible to say that these facets of precarity can *be* generalized. Similar to how Maturana and Varela talked about the concept of autopoiesis *solely* in relation to biology, I want to talk about the terms of trauma, vulnerability, and risk *solely* in relation to these six informants' experiences. These concepts have the potential to reach beyond this book and become more generalizable, but much more work needs to be done to flesh out what these concepts mean when talking through the complex web of attachments and cruel optimism that videogame production workers experience in general, and what they experience individually.

NOTES

1. According to the IGDA 2017 members' survey, roughly 80% of respondents were male, and 20% of respondents were women [Weststar et al., 2017].

2. Piotra is an alias given to Malique's former coworker. He was not sure if she would be ok with having her real name stated and had no way of contacting her to ask.

3. Samuel is an alias for Tara's brother. Since she asked that her name be anonymized, she made the point of asking that her brother's name be anonymized too after reading a draft where I did not anonymize his name.

Chapter 4

The Processual Assemblage

Getting to the Good Stuff

Elizabeth Grosz in *The Incorporeal* (2017) stresses the necessity for scholars to embrace an ontoethical view of the world around us and how we conceive of, interact with, and structure interactions and praxis. Ontoethics is composed of two component parts: ontology (onto-) and ethics (-ethics). Ontology broadly means the ways and means by which we make sense of the world around us: who we are, how we feel feelings, what and how we get attached to things (cruelly or just regularly). Additionally, ontology encompasses how we go about making sense of not only our biological body, but our metaphysical "body" insofar as our becomings, intensities, assemblages, and agencements with other bodies, both organic and nonorganic. Ethics is the far easier of the two to understand holistically, but, akin to our discussion surrounding precarity, the granular meaning and *how* we make meaning out of the concept of ethics vacillates wildly. An ethic of environmental responsibility; an ethic of cleanliness; an ethic of care; an ethic of excellence; a work ethic; an ethic of reusability; ethically sourcing material. These things all gesture towards a set of guidelines, moral or otherwise, that reinforce our choices around interactions and conceptualization, but forsake the embodied, entangled element of our interactions and collocation.

Max Weber's conceptualization of the "ideal type" (Weber, 1994) presents an interesting dichotomy to examine what an ethic might look like as part of an *onto*ethic. Weber characterizes the ideal type as a way of conceptualizing "the one-sided accentuation of one or more points of view" of which "concrete individual phenomena . . . are arranged into a unified analytical construct . . . [a] utopia [that] cannot be found empirically anywhere in reality" (Weber 1904/1949, 90). Straight away, Weber reminds us that this characterization of ideal-type-ethics that he is examining is fictional and utopic; an impossibility put forth to distract from granular, embodied experiential data. Weber stresses that we cannot hold ourselves to these logics, nor does he expect us to. Instead, Weber's goal is to highlight how entangled our own becomings and intensities of becomings are when we start to think through what an ethic might look like for us as individuals. The types of ethics that Weber is taking to task presuppose a willing, subjectivatable body and a set of subjectivating material that should impart some sort of ethical, moral, or religious guidelines. These ethics then presuppose that bodies are willing to collocate themselves within and around these ethics and that that collocation only involves the subjectivated body and the subjectivating material.

Regardless of how or where we might try and collocate ourselves on a plane of virtue, or within a monistic or dualistic point of view, true collocation is messier than simply positioning ourselves next to or in proximity to a set of virtues or to a set of truths. Therefore, ethics are messier than simple collocation as well. Instead, we must account for our interactions, interferences, and entanglements; the historical, cultural, and religious; the ontological, metaphysical, and spatiotemporal. Instead of ethics being a somewhat religious or morally guided conception, where a set of objective "good" rules, regulations, attitudes, and affects are passed down from on high, Weber is challenging us to instead break with this traditional monist viewpoint of what constitutes "good" and instead embrace almost a Nietzschean love of affects, circumstances, and impacts instead. Instead of Neitzsche's *amor fati*,[1] or love of fate (and blanket acceptance of the twists and turns of fate), maybe we can instead think of Weber's ethics in terms of *amor implicationis*: a love of entanglement. Ethics as Weber conceives of them is directly *about* our entanglements and the impact of those entanglements, not about what is moral or "good." Our actions and interactions contour and create interactions that contour and create interactions; ethics is a daisy-chain of becomings that link forward and backwards, across in/organic bodies, across time, and across space—across what Deleuze and Guattari refer to as the plane of immanence (1980). This plane is where the creation of, argument against, and acceptance/ refutation of ideas, concepts, theory, philosophy, affects, and culture occur without the limits of spatiotemporality. The plane of immanence is where I can take to task foundational philosophy of Plato without worrying about being face-to-face with him to argue or being in a certain time frame or space to undertake the weighty task of arguing with his philosophy.

If we conceive of ethics as a daisy-chaining set of becomings that rely on entanglements that are not necessarily tied to morality or objective "good," we are better prepared to recombine it with ontology and press forward to an ontoethics regarding precarities. Grosz is clear that she has actively attempted to avoid prescribing what ontoethics "is" in a theoretical sense; the entire point of *The Incorporeal* is to provide the apparatuses necessary to conceive of a more modern, more measured version of Guattari's ethicoaesthetics. New ways and means of becoming that are not tied to the capitalist socius, but, unlike Guattari's conception of utopics via ethicoaesthetics, make use of, exploit, disrupt, and create praxis that are deployable *within* the capitalist socius.

By invoking both ontology and ethics, Grosz is pushing for something that "involves an ethics that addresses not just human life in its interhuman relations, but relations between the human and an entire world, both organic and inorganic" (1). Hence why I invoked Neitzsche's *amor fati*. Nietzsche, in thinking through how human-kind can transcend to our next level of consciousness, posits that the element of utter acceptance in regard the chains of fate and eternal recurrence are vital. Nietzsche, in *Thus Spoke Zarathustra* (1883) (and to a lesser extent in *The Gay Science* [1882]) posits as a thought experiment that, if everything is infinite, are we not doomed (blessed?) to relive the same temporalities infinitely and recursively? Therefore, to transcend beyond the trappings that currently encumber us in this life, we should commit to *amor fati*, or the unconditional love and acceptance of the circumstances, situations, hardships, affects, and emotionality that contour our experiences and think beyond simply collocating ourselves to ethics, or religion, or morality. In doing so, we open ourselves up to new lines of flight within the assemblages we find ourselves imbricated, but not a Deleuzian line of flight that is one of the three lines within an assemblage that contour said assemblage. We open ourselves up to the de Landaian[2] conception of a line of flight as an operator or apparatus that transcends beyond the actual and into the virtual, where we can be more fully present to interact with conceptual fodder in the plane of immanence.

Bringing this forward into our ontoethics regarding precarity, we again must think about *amor implicationis*: what would a love of entanglement look like? I am not suggesting, nor was Nietzsche, that the love evoked in *amor fati* and *amor implicationis* should be uncritical or without ugly feelings such as jealousy, disgust, or irritation (a la Ngai, 2007). In fact, those affective states further compound what those *amors* highlight: entanglement with, and struggle for, meaning-making apparatuses. Nor should that love equate to resigned acceptance of the events happening around you. The *amor* evoked in these phrases is joie de vivre, not docile subservience. If we are to love the entanglements we find ourselves in, and if we are to think of those entanglements in terms of an ontology of ethics, we must see ourselves as active participants in those entanglements. For lack of a better phrase, we must see ourselves in the driver's seat of an actively combusting 1980s Chevy Camaro hurtling through spacetime at a million miles a second, and we must fully embrace the assemblage of daisy-chaining events, concepts, and interactions that we are implicated in here. How did we launch a Camaro into space? Why is it on fire while in space? Why is our terminal velocity a million miles per second? All of these things work as discrete events to describe a spatiotemporal point in time, of course. But when examined together, though, we are presented with a rich assemblage of becomings that interlock, build upon each other, and contour, forwards and backwards, where we collocate ourselves on the plane of immanence as well as where we collocate ourselves in the moment of occurrence. And this is what Grosz is pushing for when talking about ontoethics: the full embrace of where we are in the moment, where we come from, where the events that have led to this moment are, and where our potentiality stretches out to. All as a methodology and active approach to reimagining the apparatuses through which we make meaning and make entanglements.

If we are to take anything away from this text, I want it to be that, to affect change in game development and to start to make inroads to alleviating crunch, detangling ourselves from precarities, further contouring what precarities are, and better understanding our own cruelly optimistic attachments, we must change our viewpoints and scope for two things. The first, and arguably the most important, is: where does our conception of multiplicative precarities locate itself in terms of an ontoethical view of videogame production? What does an assemblage look like where precarities can collocate themselves with *amor implicationis*? Can the implications present in the precarities we have discussed actually be loved and embraced in such a way that that love doesn't just become *another* element of cruel optimism? How do we prevent overdeterministic scoping when thinking through where and with what these concepts (precarities, ontology, ethics) collocate themselves on the plane of immanence? The second is how can we move beyond rote, deterministic interventions, or overly idealized, utopic interventions and instead start to think and act in an ontoethical way? What would an ontoethics of unionization and collective action look like? Are these activities even *possible* if we follow the line of reasoning that Grosz lays out in *The Incorporeal*?

If we lean into the theoretical diligence we have given to the concepts that inform and contour the capitalist socius' implications in creating the material-discursive circumstances that we find ourselves embroiled in in videogame production, we have already done the hard work of collocation. We know (approximately—this is the granular element of collocation; "we" is a stand-in for me, you, them, etc.) where we are, we know the daisy chains that are flowering forward and backwards that imbricate us in these current circumstances, and we know, conceptually and theoretically, how and why the negative things that I have felt and that my informants have felt and that I have outlined are functioning and *why* they are functioning. At least in enough depth that we can start thinking about ontoethics as a system of applied/appliable discursive possible circumstances; as lines of flight, ways of deterritorializing and reterritorializing the assemblages we are imbricated in. Deleuze and Guattari in *Anti-Oedipus* (1980) define lines of flight as "the abstract line, the line of flight or deterritorialization according to which they change in nature and connect with other multiplicities" (9–10). Lines of flight are an agent of change insomuch as they are elements capable of collapsing different multiplicities on a plane of consistency into one cohesive set of agencements. But not change insomuch as they statically operate on an element in a certain spatial or temporal frame. They operate across multiplicities to foster new potentialities and new becomings that will render new dimensions and possibilities for those potentialities. So that begs the final question of this section: what are the lines of flight necessary to traverse the potentialities present in our current ways and means of conceptualizing of videogame production across to a new ontoethical praxical movement within videogame production?

ONTOETHICS AND ETHICOAESTHETICS: THE CONFUSING QUESTION OF UTOPIA

It is important to address the utopics that might be associated with ontoethics before moving onto actually conceptualizing what ontoethics could be in videogame production. To do so, we need to take a step back from simply looking at videogame production and instead conceptualize within the wider frame of the capitalist socius as a whole as much as I am want to do since it does not necessarily foreground granularity and embodied experience. Within the capitalist socius, we know that there are certain lines of flight, or methods of egress, from the negative thoughts, feelings, imbrications, agencements we find ourselves in. Chief among those lines of flight are Guattari's ethicoaesthetics. Ethicoaesthetics are Guattari's version of utopia without the perfectionism and without as much idealism that utopics are usually given. I have invoked Guattari at multiple points in this work, and I would be remiss to not address his ideas of ethicoaesthetics as alternatives to integrated world capitalism since IWC was a component part for conceptualizing our current assemblage of videogame production. Ethicoaesthetics are experimental objects that act as ways of circumventing formal power structures by way of creating what Guattari, in *Chaosmosis* (1995), refers to as the third Assemblage: the processual Assemblage. This assemblage contains "unprecedented, unforeseen and unthinkable qualities of being" (106) which are collocated alongside things like art.[3] Guattari says that this assemblage "No longer [aggregates] and [territorializes] (as in the first illustration of Assemblage) or [autonomises] and [transcendentalises] (as in the second), they are now crystallised in singular and dynamic constellations which envelop and make constant use of these two modes of subjective and machinic production" (108). If we understand the territorialized assemblage to contain both the tribal and despotic sociuses, and the deterritorialized assemblage to contain the capitalist socius and trace amounts of the despot and tribal, then we can conceive of the processual assemblage as part of an emerging ethicoaesthetic socius, based on what Guattari envisioned in a postcapitalist socius. This ethicoaesthetic socius will be enlivened by postindividualism, and movement towards reorganization around central semiotic markers instead of the highly individualized subjectivation that we see as part of the autopoietic process in the capitalist socius.

Ethicoaesthetics can only exist within this third assemblage, where subjectivational and machinic logics no longer are *solely* dictated by capital generation. Meaning, since we are firmly ensconced in late-stage capitalism currently, ethicoaesthetics that circumvent the power structures we are operating within may prove impossible to access immediately or without leaning into schizoanalysis/becoming-schizophrenic, as per Deleuze and Guattari in *Anti-Oedipus* (1983). O'Sullivan (2010), however, says that we are currently seeing a semi-embryonic processual assemblage forming, and, arguably, has already begun the process of "passing through" the second assemblage. But, that "passing through" is not a clean pass. The third assemblage's passage through the second means that, as the third propagates and creates new agencements in the form of autopoietic nuclei (systems of subjectivation that are no longer overcoded straight from the capitalist socius but instead almost circle back to a savage organization around central, community-focused semiotic meaning-making), the processual assemblage opens itself up to being carrion-bird picked by the deterritorialized assemblage. This means that, as pieces are picked off the processual assemblage by the deterritorialized assemblage, those elements are then added to the deterritorialized assemblage's autopoietic structure. These then can be monetized and involved in the process of subjectivating bodies to conform to productive processes, which is where we see videogame production's problem with representation discussed earlier. This presents a worrisome possible hole in the utopics that Guattari is invoking through ethicoaesthetics.

As we discussed earlier, the capitalist socius need for forms of autopoietic subjectivation means that, as new cultural signifiers become prescient, the socius will be seeking to incorporate those form signifiers into productive overcoding. And herein lies the problem of the processual assemblage's passage through the deterritorialized assemblage. Guattari saw ethicoaesthetics as a new line of flight: "rather than moving in the direction of reductionist modifications which simplify the complex . . . [working] towards its complexification, its processual enrichment, towards the consistency of its virtual lines of bifurcation and differentiation, in short towards its ontological heterogeneity" (1995, 61). Ethicoaesthics are not meant to simplify the world around us, or act as mediations of the world around us. They are meant to radically change the way that we perceive of the world, akin to taking psychedelics: egress from the industrial grays and browns that Deleuze, Guattari, Weber, and Foucault envision the world being colored in and move towards a multidimensional, multicolored, lush new aesthetic focused outside of processual becomings that make up the subjectivating elements of the capitalist socius.

As I discussed in the first chapter about theorizations of how passion, precarity, and cruel optimism collide in videogame production, those theorizations forsake the embodied, granular bodies in the systems they are examining. Similarly, Guattari forsakes the embodied non/human bodies at work in these assemblages. There is very little in the way of a conception of the personal and the molecular when Guattari talks through what an ethicoaesthetic assemblage might look like; just that it is inherently schizophrenic, and processes, systems, and assumedly bodies, are "crystallized" into their own systems. O'Sullivan says that the processual assemblage is supposed to be postindividualistic regarding taking back our own subjectivation. But, where does that leave those of us stuck in this bastard stage where the deterritorialized socius is carrion-birding the processual assemblage? How do we action these future-forward theorizations while also being tied to the immediate, material-discursive trappings of the capitalist socius? The problem with these types of theorizations lies in how they handle that temporal bubble and the embodied emotionality that we can't . . . quite . . . theorize about in the future since we are stuck in the present. The affective, the emotional, the entangled and entanglements that we cannot quite verbalize; the feelings in the pit of our stomachs; the itch at the back of our heads. Guattari's ethicoaesthetics presuppose a certain type of body that will commit to the same sort of love as Nietzsche's *amor fati*, except instead of circumstances, it is unbridled love for the supplanting of institutionally sanctioned knowledge-making and overcoding. It presupposes a type of body that will engage in subterfuge, commit to ways of being that are considered "crazy" or incompatible with life and being in its current state.

This presupposition cannot and does not account for bodies stuck in the middle: the bodies that want change, want new ways of being and becoming, but in order to usher in that change, must sacrifice their lives, the lives of those around them (family, partners, etc.), and the lives of those not involved in wanting to usher in the processual assemblage. Since we are, unfortunately, tied to the whims and means of the capitalist socius for the rote day-to-day, second-to-second ways of subsisting, we have to play by those rules: we have to generate capital to live, we have to sacrifice our moral (ethicoaesthetic) self to allow the socius to subjectivate us in such a way that we can sustain ourselves, our loved ones, and our communities. And herein lies the problem. There is no code, no theorization, no handbook for how to navigate actualizing the type of body that Guattari presupposes. I certainly do not have the answers for what to do to help usher in the processual assemblage. We can certainly quit our jobs, try and go back to the savage socius' ways of communal, tribal living, and we can actively try and circumvent the need to engage with the capitalist socius in an effort to encourage others to do similarly. But, this cannot account for factors of corporal control that would immediately become blockages to this type of regression into the savage socius. And we *see* aspects of corporal control, and of cultural control, every time a commune is mentioned in parlance. Just look at the hippie communes of Twin Oaks in Virginia and The Farm in Tennessee. Documentaries and write-ups of these communes detail police and governmental intervention and violence to usurp what they were doing. Not to mention the overall tone that most of the documentaries and write-ups take regarding the matter. These communities are treated as fascinators; things that the average person would never engage with or do but would gladly consume as part of a subjectivation course of what "crazy" or "worthless/nonproductive" bodies look like.

And herein lies the problematicity of utopics that I have alluded to. Guattari is assuming that the bodies active in, and responsible for, ushering in the third assemblage, and with it, a new ethicoaesthetic ontology, have the capabilities, affects, and concepts (and conceptual personae) amenable to a steady, processual imbrication. There is also nothing spoken about the potential problematicity of those engaging with an ushering in of the third assemblage abandoning or forsaking the cause due to guilt, or jealousy, or the very same schizophrenic entanglements that Deleuze and Guattari spend so much time valorizing. For as much as Deleuze and Guattari argue for schizoanalysis and schizophrenic arrangements, there is surprisingly little regarding how, under current medical and governmental operating regimes, those of us with mental illnesses, or debilitating physical illnesses, are supposed to either usher in a generation of schizoanalysis or use those dis/abilities to reorder the world around us. Similarly to Foucault's biopower,[4] or how to effectively subjugate large numbers of similar bodies, the theorization of broken or othered bodies is rife ground for imagining a different operating environment to what we currently have, or for describing how our current institutions are inherently broken, but those bodies are *well often* forsaken once a point is made about what a world that operates based on those differences. The case is no different when conceptualizing ethicoaesthetics; different and othered bodies are subjectized, operationalized, and then lost somewhere in the shuffle of present to future. It is partially this irresponsibility in theorization that further allows for the precarities that I spoke about earlier to exist and propagate.

ASSEMBLY IN THE PROCESSUAL ASSEMBLAGE:
NEARNESS, SUFFERING, AND POLITICS . . .

I want to take this opportunity to return to one of the themes of this piece and possible reconfigure some of the assumptions about it for the positive: collocation. Or, for our purposes now, assembly. Assembly is how I would like to think through the element of how we find "our people" that ethicoaesthetics do not cover. Assembly is a possible way in which in-betweeners and those of us who cannot radicalize because of our imbrications with capital, or commitments to those who depend on us for support can still form our own protoprocessual assemblages and assist in usurping the capitalist socius. Butler (2015) talks about assembly in component parts of nearness and belonging. Hardt and Negri (2019) seek to reorganize collection and collocation in terms of politicality and define assembly as something moving from a "*politics* of plurality" into an "*ontology machine*" of plurality (69, emphasis my own). Both Butler and Hardt and Negri are working towards understanding aspects that constitute assembly. For Butler, those aspects are focused more on nearness and proximity and what types of actions assembly generally inhabit. For Hardt and Negri, it is the politicality and understanding the cohesive dynamics inherent to assembly. Both contributions to understanding assembly directly correlate with the missing element of the processual assemblage: in/organic bodies and embodied experience. How do we collocate with people who are keen to push towards a shared understanding or a shared vision? Where do we find, and for that matter even articulate, nearness in terms of in/organic bodies that are seeking the same end goals as us? Where and how can we, while working within the material-discursive confines of the capitalist socius, articulate new ethicoaesthetic movements that both sabotage and refamiliarize routines inherent to capital generation in such a way that they even *allow* us to find closeness without it becoming a Berlantian nightmare?

I want to quickly differentiate between "assembly" versus "assemblage" since I am using both in this section. "Assembly" as Hardt and Negri say is not invoked as a "theory of assembly or a detailed analysis of any specific practice of assembly. Instead, we approach the concept transversally and show how it resonates with a broad web of political principles and practices . . . Assembly is a lens through which to recognize new democratic political possibilities" (XXI). The act of assembly, and the politics of assembly, are present *in* assemblages, but the verbiage and connotations are different. Similarly for Butler, she is theorizing on the dynamics of groups and how the performance of assembly can be constituted in terms of affect, spatiality, and temporality. The component parts of assembly that Hardt and Negri and Butler are talking about the parts I want to take forward to continue theorizing on the processual assemblage. As I said at the start of this section, the processual assemblage and ethicoaesthetics are lacking a clear understanding or articulation of where and how in/organic bodies fit into these structures, which is where these scholars' work becomes integral.

I want to note before I start that I am not necessarily interested in the constituency that Butler engages with in the opening pages of *Notes Toward a Performative Theory of Assembly* (2015) that acknowledges what Mouffe and Laclau describe as "constituent exclusion." At this point in the type of theorization I am attempting in this chapter, I do not particularly care about the semantics behind who is and is not being "included" or who is being demarcated against straight away. I want to include everyone who works in some form or facet in videogame production that is disadvantaged and wants to see the type of creative process that the processual assemblage would allow in these articulations. Streamers and content creators, coders, sound designers, modelers, animators, lighting designers, voice actors, administrative staff, social media managers, community managers, quality assurance testers, hobbyist game makers, modders, hackers, so on. The task of determining who is and is not eligible for unions and collective action, and who can and cannot be a part of this aspect of processual assembly is another project in and of itself; one I have struggled with through multiple publications and I feel like I am still no closer to solving because of just how unwieldy those questions are.

What I do want to focus on, however, is the quandary for work like this that Butler presents. (Co)locating bodies in proximity to an object of attachment is so important for articulating portions of contingent theory through which I draw out the praxic elements that I discuss in the final chapter. However, there is little credence given to nearness and proximity in much of the literature of Deleuze and Guattari. In fact, spatiality of bodies is something that they actively theorize away from at times it seems. Butler however, through Emmanuel Levinas, articulates that "belonging" is as multifaceted as our definition of precarities is and just as important when considering assembly; one that is necessary when we start to think through what a processual assemblage might contain or be undergirded by. Levinas insists, as Butler says, "we are bound to those we do not know, and even those we did not choose, could never have chosen, and that these obligations are, strictly speaking, precontractual" (107). While Levinas may articulate this sense of intense belong and bonded milieus, Butler drills down into the bedrock of this sentiment to say that the primacy of the "other" in Levinas' writing buries the "self"; in other words, the emphasis put on our belong and nearness with communities that we cannot choose, or cannot be known to, or cannot relocate away from does not leave room for ethics of care. There is no room in this notion of collocation to self-preserve. Though I am not partial to Butler's reduction of in/human connection to simply "living processes that exceed human form" (108) simply because it creates too nebulous a net through which to collocate, the refutation of Levinas in this way is important for understanding how, within our current articulated existences, we can start forming our own embryonic processual assemblages; processual bubbles, if you will.

At the end of the day, the milieus we inhabit, the assemblages we articulate and ensconce ourselves in, and the agencements present in these socialities are only possible because, as Butler says, we are tied together through nonhuman, inorganic processes through which our lives are dictated. Labor, and the valuation of labor, is one such process. Industrial and institutional knowledge and foundationalism is another. We understand and articulate social cues, cultural cues, eventual cues, and processual cues in a distinctly human way; meaning, we process the information, sensations, affects, libidinal energies, and becomings that are present in a circumstance, and we make our own inferences about what those things mean and how we should react. Like a fingerprint, our interpretation and process of these things is innately our own. But through these interpretations, we can find nearness and collocation with others whose interpretations converge with ours. In the most base form, neighborhood interest groups exemplify this type of collocation. Close in proximity, but possibly not close in terms of culture, affective state, finance, or a multitude of other multitudes. However, a common goal is shared: upkeep and watchfulness in accordance with a space. There are clashes within the group, factions, differing opinions, differing subgoals, differing convictions, and even nonparticipants or antiparticipants, but ultimately, the group is an assembly, and the agencements of that assembly are concerned with making sure that the space that they all inhabit is safe, looked after, and kept in consideration.

But, as Butler also says, not all these articulations are pleasant, and by the nature of what I am doing here, and what you are doing here, we are opening ourselves up to the nameless, Levinassian "Other." As Butler articulates, our proximity to and closeness to other bodies may end in our persecution and suffering. Levinas valorizes this suffering as something that strengthens the bond experienced, and that the survival of the group should trump individualism—to the point of suffering. However, if we hope to move towards a processual socius, we must consider where individualism and suffering fits into our articulation of nearness and proximity. Revisiting Guattari's articulation of the processual assemblage means that we must conceive of this—of *our*—assembly as constellations of individualism (articulations assemble as "crystallised in singular and dynamic constellations which envelop and make constant use of these two modes of subjective and machinic production") (108). This means that, as we find nearness with other in/organic bodies, we must run a fine line that incorporates individualism ontologically and processually into the bigger picture of goals as that individualism being one of many stars in the sky. We must avoid having "main character syndrome" where we (the very individual, granular, embodied "we"—you and I, dear reader) are locked into thinking that the actions, circumstances, and becomings that we undertake and wrestle with are given special credence because they are happening to *us*. Instead, we must recognize our own individual ontology and articulations and we must coalesce with other individual bodies to create a starfield where our individualism contributes to a common goal: an assembly.

Hardt and Negri (2019) in *Assembly* are approaching assembly from a similar fashion insofar as they are concerned with the people taking part *in* the assembly and how we can further theorize about assemblage in more generative ways. Hardt and Negri characterize assembly, and the multitudes that inhabit those milieu, as something that

> [flows] sometimes in full view and then descends for periods into subterranean channels, but together they nonetheless generate an accumulation of practices and subjectivity. Their flows flows deposit geological layers of a sedimentary social being. We need to focus for a moment on these discontinuous and multiple flows that characterize a plural ontology of politics. (67)

Something that Butler does not articulate as fully or as directly as Hardt and Negri is that the types of groups we are talking about are inherently political in nature. Any time we talk about labor processes, capital generation, and the semantics of life in a hostile system, it is political. The processual assemblage, processual bubbles, milieus that unfold, agencements that contour and characterize these spaces, and the rhizomatic approach that these spaces operate under to make use of the libidinal energies that are flowing through them all are all political in nature. So, when we speak about the processual assemblage and possible forms of assembly that direct bodies towards that organization, we are inherently invoking politics of the body[5] alongside component ethical forms of environment, science, material, technology, etc. In other words, we are inherently talking about in/organic bodies' ability to access spaces; entering, staying upon, inhabiting, exploring. We are also talking about bodies' right to becomings and intensities—are these bodies allowed to change and grow alongside the processual assemblage? Or are we locked in a unidirectional growth? We are also talking about bodies' rights to learning and technicity—are all bodies privileged with the same access and equity to systems of creation within the processual assemblage? Or, again, are we locked into rote roles and responsibilities; a hierarchical structure. If we take Guattari at his word regarding ethicoaesthetic growth and the utopics inherent in that kind of growth, we must return to the sentiment about individualism being a constellation. Guattari and O'Sullivan *intend* for there to be renegotiations and becomings within and throughout the processual assemblage.

Hardt and Negri, in furthering the "political" aspect of assembly, say that the "pluralism of subjectivities, multiple modes of temporality, and a wide variety of modes of struggle . . . emerge from different traditions and express different objectivities, together form a powerful swarm held together by cooperative logic" (69). Hardt and Negri provide us with a way of characterizing the cohesive agents that Butler did not in the form of cooperative logics. While Butler was able to articulate the affective and proximal aspect of assembly through Levinas, the cohesive agent there was not an autonomous agent. Meaning, the thing that was holding together the assembly that Butler articles through Levinas was not something that the members of those groups could fully decide on for themselves. Hardt and Negri imply that there must be some sort of cohesive, cooperative logic behind an assembly which is dictated on an individual basis but together form a cooperative goal. We see this in the general assembly of what we have come to think of as the processual assemblage.

Another important element of assembly that Hardt and Negri articulate here is that assemblies are not necessarily always *da sein*—they are not always in direct existence, or even public existence. Going back to Butler though, when we find nearness and closeness with a group of people, the affects that those entwinements predicate do not disappear or cease to exist. They are articulated on the plane of immanence as conceptual fodder. They are embedded in memory and ontologies. They are remembered, reviled, struggled with, loved. This directly undergirds what the processual assemblage stands for. The processual assemblage cannot be thought of as one static, evergreen thing. It is a series of assemblies; group becomings, intensities and libinal flows of energy; torrential outpourings in public spaces; meetings in back rooms, hidden from scrutiny. There is nothing static or one-way about the processual assemblage or how the processual assemblage is being ushered in; it is the ultimate example of becoming.

All of this explication to further instantiate: the aspect of bodies in assemblages, and by proxy of bodies, assembly, is an instrumental part of what is missing from theorization around ushering in the processual assemblage and any discussion around ethicoaesthetics. O'Sullivan helps us to best understand the articulation of where in/organic bodies (by way of individualism) fit into the processual assemblage by reminding us that the processual assemblage is postindividualistic and instead relies of constellations of individualism pushing their own libinal energies and becomings into furthering a group becoming. Butler and Hardt and Negri provide us an important set of terminology in terms of assembly and what we can expect and *should* expect from the bodies who are in proximity with one another, contouring these eventual becomings. It is not always utopic, it is not always positive; sometimes the proximal intensities bodies will find themselves imbricated in are violent, territorial, and chocked full of ugly emotions a la Ngai: jealousy, envy, apathy, hate, indifference. That does not necessarily mean that the assemblage that those affects and becomings are happening in is any less important or potentially impactful. They are considerations that must be made, and contours that must be assessed as we ourselves figure out what the processual assemblage "looks" like in videogame production.

... In Videogames

As a reminder, none of this theorization is just native to videogame production; as a society, we are facing an uphill struggle to usher in the processual assemblage given the absolutely staggering stranglehold the deterritorialized socius has. But, given the powerful semiotic and cultural subjectivational capacity of videogame production under the capitalist socius, I think that videogame production could be a case study (or at least crash test) for potential lines of flight. Additionally, how we assemble, and the necessities of assembly are not native to videogame production either. The aspects that Butler talks about regarding closeness and proximity extend well beyond this group and inhabit *any* assembly where a processual assemblage might be involved. Same for Hardt and Negri. The flexibility of assembly, and the cohesive aspects of assembly undergird and contour any discussion where the processual assemblage comes up. Without proximity and nearness, and without the cooperative and flexible elements of assembly, the processual assemblage as we understand it (the constellation of crystalized individuals, according to Guattari) is impossible. But via these theorizations, we could figure out, from a high level, what onotoethics might look like: what are we hoping to accomplish? What bodies count for our conception of who our ontoethics applies to? Where is our *amor implicatus* leading us?

As of now, the utopics found in ethicoaesthetics are inaccessible via our current theoretical structure. However, can we not use the same tools as the capitalist socius to help usher in the processual assemblage? How can we perform our own form of subterfuge on the capitalist socius and carrion-bird old or discarded parts of the socius and reinvigorate them for our own movements? And can we not at least in part address the issues above regarding dis/abled bodies being forsook in the shuffle from theory to praxis? How can we articulate ourselves in nearness with others and collaboratively come to terms with a cooperative logic for assembly? I believe that this is where ontoethics can bridge the theoretical gap from, well, theory into praxis and provide us with a way of taking the embedded, material structures of unions and collective action and collocate them in the plane of immanence.

NOTES

1. See *The Gay Science (1886)* and *Thus Spoke Zarathustra (1883)* for a full explication of what *amor fati* is; it is multifaceted beyond just my conception of "a love of fate," but this project is not quite the right place to explicate *amor fati* in full force in modern parlance.

2. See *Intensive Science and Virtual Philosophy* (2002) for a fuller explication on de Landa's conception of lines of flight. Suffice it to say, he recontextualizes Deleuze and Guattari's conception of a line of flight as something that in/organic bodies are capable of doing (similar to what Deleuze and Guattari reference as desiring-bodies), instead of being a rather nebulous support structure of an assemblage that sees in/organic bodies both imbricated and not imbricated in the support of the assemblage.

3. For a deep treatment of the entanglement of art, the unthinkable/unactionable, and chaos as both ontological tools and tools of egress from our "normal" environments, see *Chaos, Territory, and Art* by Elizabeth Grosz (2008), *Chaosmosis* by Felix Guattari (1995) and "Guattari's Aesthetic Paradigm: From the Folding of the Finite/Infinite Relation to Schizoanalytic Metamodelisation" by Simon O'Sullivan (2010). These texts provide detailed exegesis about what makes art transgressive, what about art is chaotic insofar as its ability to pervert the world around it and create new affects, concepts (on a plane of immanence), and entanglements across culture. They provide the basis through which we can understand Guattari's conceptualization of the three Assemblages (territorialized, deterritorialized, and processual), and where we can collocate the ontological and material-discursive pinnings that allow for the theorization of ethicoaesthetics as Guattari does.

4. For definitional work around biopower, see *A History of Sexuality* (1990) by Foucault. Simply put, biopower is a technology of power that allows for mass control over populations, races, sexualities, etc. and axiomatizes bodily function in terms of labor, be it physical, immaterial, affective, support, etc.

5. For a fuller understanding of the depth and breadth of body politics I am talking about, see *Bodily Natures* by Stacy Alaimo, *Body/Poltiics: Women and the Discourses of Science* by Mary Jacobus, Evelyn Fox Keller, and Sally Shuttleworth, *Volatile Bodies* by Elizabeth Grosz.

Chapter 5

Ontoethical Praxis

Judith Butler (2015) in *Notes Toward a Performative Theory of Assembly* says the following regarding proximity and parasociality in terms of where *we* locate ourselves in conjunction with social issues. Butler asks about ethical quandaries that images and accounts of war and suffering elicit: "is what is happening so far away from me that I can bear no responsibility for it? Is what is happening so close to me that I cannot bear having to take responsibility for it? If I myself did make this suffering, am I still in some sense responsible for it?" (101). As I covered in the previous chapter, proximal identifications imbricate us in these types of suffering; as Levinas covers, suffering is a shared dynamic. However, the associated affects of suffering such as grief, precarities, and trauma can be very individual and can be a basis on which we start to articulate our own set of ethical imbrications within the processual assemblage.

Butler also locates ethics, again via Levinas, as a standard of relationality within the cells and milieus we inhabit: "I find that I am my relation to the 'you' whose life I seek to preserve, and without that relation, this 'I' becomes undone in its ethical relation to the 'you,' which means that there is a very specific mode of being dispossessed that makes ethical relationality possible" (110). This means that, as we move towards an understanding of nearness in a processual, postcapitalist, postindividual assemblage, if we go with Levinas' articulation of ethics, and what I spoke about in the third chapter about vulnerability within collocation, we can see that ethics is not necessarily a code of conduct, or a set of rules, or even a social contract with others. Ethics, instead, is multiplicative articulations of all of those things alongside the subjectivations of the assemblage. Meaning, ethics does not *just* have to be thought of in terms of dictating correct or incorrect actions, allegiances, social cues, etc. Ethics and ethical considerations should also be considered on ability to commit to them and the longeval effects that those ethics might have in relation to our embodied, current existences.

So, what, then, might a praxis look like that accounts for the immediate and the embodied? For the bodies "in the middle"? For bodies that desperately seek a new way of being, but cannot go join a videogame production commune? While it may seem somewhat antithetical to talk about using the capitalist socius' own tools against it given the rather stark image I have painted of it as being something that, without fail, will attempt to monetize and incorporate actions against it, there is a sliver of hope. The processual assemblage and the ethicoaesthetic socius can both be characterized as concepts (in the plane of immanence) that require "schizophrenic" thinking to actualize. And if we follow how Deleuze and Guattari talk about schizophrenia as being something so antithetical to the operating systems of the world that it requires institutionalization, then it would follow that, to start ushering in a new way of thinking, becoming, and being, then we have to start thinking so far outside of current operating parameters that we risk someone sending us on a vacation somewhere with grippy socks. Which, in short, means that we start thinking of ways to subvert the capitalist socius in ways that echo how it currently operates: find ways of using it for *our* immediate autopoietic needs, discard the systems we make use of, then, in true Nietzschian fashion, make recursive use of those systems to, again, subvert the socius once it does its due diligence of weaponizing *our* new set of agencements. In effect, we are looking to grind the hyperproductiveness and hypermasculinity of videogame production to a halt; no more valorizing overwork and bodily harm, no more work environments like Riot (see: D'Anastasio, 2018) or Blizzard's Bill Cosby suite,[1] and no more opaque remuneration or advancement structures like my informants (and many others from the literature I have referenced throughout this book) have experienced. In other words: we find systems within our current assemblage that can experience short-circuiting or sabotage in regard to creating "productive" bodies, such as my informant in the previous section who fought for a recovery room and then ushered in a new ethic of care that the company did not want but in the end took credit for. We exploit those systems to create ethics of care and ethics of kindness that have been absent in videogame production: caring for ourselves, one another, and caring for the product we are making.

These actions are already in effect to an extent in videogame production: my informants from my third chapter, for example. The people who lent their voices to this book *and* the people who were gracious with their time but not comfortable being spot lit all represent direct praxic elements within videogame production: change starts with a conversation. Change starts when people say "this isn't right, how can I change it." There are other areas in videogame production where these ethics are in effect to some extent: Tanya Short of Kitfox Games. She has gone on record many times to say that Kitfox does not believe in crunch, and no one is required to work crunch there regardless of the circumstances. In fact, workers at Kitfox are actively *discouraged* from working crunch. She also co-heads Pixells, which is a Montreal-based inclusive, women-and-queer-focused games initiative that provides a place to make games, workshop games, find communion and networking opportunities, with the ultimate goal of making games that are, and change games to be, more inclusive. And of course, there are videogame production union and resource groups like Independent Workers of Great Britain's Game Workers branch, Syndicat de Travailleurs et Travailleuses du Je Video, Le Rassemblement Inclusif de Jeu Video, Union syndicale Solidaires, Syndicat National du Jeu Video, Solidares Informatique Jeu Video, More Perfect Unions, and Game Workers Alliance. But none of these bodies in game production work from the same system or set of understandings, which means that, even though these bodies have similar aims, they are achieving vastly different results. For example, France has very robust union support, and quite a few studios in France are either part of these unions or actively make use of collective action to fight the precarities that I have gone over earlier.

If we refer back to our initial positing of what ontoethics might be, we need to remember *amor implicationis*: an unabashed, unafraid love of entanglement. We also need to be aware of where we are collocating ourselves with these entanglements. Ontoethics, for us, means (at least partially) the full embrace of where we are in the moment, where we come from, where the events that have led to this moment are, and where our potentiality stretches out to. All as a methodology and active approach to reimagining the apparatuses through which we make meaning and make entanglements. It is the "reimagining" part that I want to focus on here. We know that the current systems in place in videogame production are exploitative and ultimately only serve the capitalist socius' pursuit of autopoiesis. Based on this, I want to at least put down on paper a few basic problem areas that ontoethics can be deployed in:

1. Crunch.

Problems: who is responsible for the daisy chain of events that lead to crunch? What bodies are making decisions about the flows of work that end up necessitating crunch? If we cannot collocate blame with a certain job title/level of seniority/system/body, then what discrete entanglements are leading to crunch?

Ontoethical Approach: how do we go about short-circuiting the institutional circuitry present in perpetuating crunch? What would an ethic of production look like that does not valorize overwork and "battlescarring" from crunch?

2. The operationalization of passion.

Problems: why is passion being weaponized/used as a policing measure/ used as a meritocratic measure? What about passion as a concept (on the plane of immanence) makes it so convenient to exploit? Where is passion being collocated alongside attachments?

Ontoethical Approach: what would an ethic of production look like that doesn't subsist on operationalizing passion as a way of extracting excess labor from workers? What would an ethic of production look like that's slow and careful?

3. Encroaching precarities.

Problems: as demonstrated in the previous chapter, the aforementioned two problems create splinters, or opportunities for splinters, of affect in the form of multiplicative precarities such as trauma, risk, and vulnerability. These precarities are *born* from the aforementioned two problems, but compound, multiply, and exacerbate those problems.

Ontoethical Approach: what would an ethic of production look like that actively acknowledges that these preacarities (and many more unmentioned simply due to scope and informants' experience) exist and proliferate in game production? What would an ethic of production look like that works to short-circuit the nodes where bodies collocate with precarities?

4. Cohesiveness across games work that is moving towards how Guattari conceptualized postindividualism in the processual assemblage.

Problems: as I discussed earlier, there are instances where some of these ontoethical approaches are already in place. But they are not cohesive and they do not have floors or ceilings for what bodies can participate, where, when, or how. Collective action and unionization in videogame production in its current form are *vastly* different in functionality, access, and cultural relevance.

Onotoethical Approach: what would an ethic of production look like that embraces togetherness; joined-ness? What would an ethic or production look like that embraces historically relevant unionization and collective action processes that the capitalist socius actually *could not* absorb? What would an ethic of production look like that is redolent of pre-Thatcher English industrial workers?

5. Enculturation of nonwhite, nonmale bodies via the processes that Guattari refers to as homogeneity and gender renegotiation.

Problem: as I touched on in the first chapter, game development is still a primarily heterosexual, white, male endeavor. This is due in large part to the subjectivation process of videogame production seeking to make actively interchangeable bodies that do not hamper the production cycle. As Guattari talks about with gender renegotiation, homogeneity in enculturation spaces, or semiotic spaces, means that the socius is doing less work realigning bodies to productive cycles.

Ontoethical Approach: what would an ethic of production look like that is not predicated on gender renegotiation and is, in fact, an equitable work-place? What would a resurgence of personal games creation and not-for-profit game creation look like today as opposed to when it was in its heyday in the early 2010s?

The identification of these problems and proposed ontoethical approaches are predicated, again, on fully embracing the entanglements and concepts that make up the current agencements we find ourselves in. The ontoethical turn, though, can only happen once these problems' imbrication in the capitalist socius becomes apparent. Once those imbrications are clear, only then can we actually go about assembling our new apparatuses of meaning-making and entanglement-making: our ontoethics. I want to take the following sections to highlight, more in depth, two of these situations: short-circuiting crunch, and cohesion across games work. These two issues present entanglements that are a bit deeper than just "stop doing crunch" or "get together with other unions/collective action bodies to make a more cohesive plan." The follow-ing sections will recontextualize these problems and offer some very cursory ways that we might start to take them apart in the pursuit of helping usher in the processual assemblage.

THE POSSIBILITY OF SHORT-CIRCUITING CRUNCH VIA SHORT-CIRCUITING PARASOCIALITY

I have already covered what crunch is, the reasons that crunch manifests, and the reasons that crunch has become this perverse mark of honor across videogame production. We know that crunch, in its basest form, is a subjec-tivation measure, and a way of extracting surplus labor for no remuneration. It is disguised as "having passion for the medium," and payment is given in having proximity to the cultural cache that comes with making games. I believe that collocating where the breakdowns in institutional circuitry are that end up forcing crunch, be it poor management, having to fudge timelines to keep investors happy, or breakdowns in team structure, are all beyond the scope of an introductory ontoethical intervention. However, I do believe that there are some discrete entanglements that we *can* pick apart in an attempt to short-circuit crunch. One of those, of course, is the belief that unremunerated crunch is somehow an act of valor and is one to be applauded. Meritocratic mobility does not reward this type of passion unless it is collocated with a certain body: in most cases, straight, white, and male. That is simply a symptom of the spaces that game production has historically taken place in and the bodies that game production has been made for and continues to be made for. I will speak about gender renegotiation later, which is an important part of the subjectivation process in videogame production, but for the moment, let us leave meritocracy at the fact that it is not a gender/color/race/sexual orientation-blind strategy for rewarding work and effort. As Guattari says of becoming-woman, most spaces of inculcation are spaces of homogeneity: the spaces where subjectivation take place are better suited to having mostly the same type of body, type of personality, and type of worker. This way, the process of production does not as readily breakdown, and bodies are much more willing to fit the form of being-productive.

But we also know that that is not the only subjectivation measure that crunch allows for. I want to take this section to dig into how, within the capitalist socius, crunch is not just a subjectivation measure a la Mike Epps' infamous proclamation that, if you are not prepared to work at least 60 hours a week, you will not last. Crunch also acts as another measure of collocation that compliments cruel optimism. Or, rather, adds another layer of complexity to it in that, this collocation is no longer a one-to-one equation of you-to-object of attachment. Crunch, in the age of post-Gamer Gate social media, allows for a unique kind of cruelly optimistic attachment where the workers that we have focused on so far are now simply *vehicles* for others' cruelly optimistic attachments. Specifically, if we follow current trends of crunch (including studios outright lying about not making workers work crunch only to find out that they forced workers to sometimes work 100+ hour weeks), workers are not just collocating next to their object of attachments (videogames/ culture/production); they are also forced to collocate with consumers' objects of attachment. Consumers, at the same time, want finished, perfect, polished games, but they also want those games without delays, without consideration for the people working behind the scenes, and without any impacting factors aside from "this game is now coming out ahead of schedule." And because of how pervasive and ubiquitous social media (especially Twitter) has become, developers are often no longer provided any modicum of privacy to hide behind. Whereas once, you would only see game company's social medias being brigaded when they announced delays or complications, now we see it happening to individual developers when games are pushed back. Game developers are now being opened up to continual abuse from disgruntled fans even when nothing "official" has happened that would generally generate community response. Again, the ubiquity of social media has opened individual developers up to becoming, in effect, a steppingstone for gamers' own cruel optimism. If they cannot affect change or have their message heard across the main social media presence of a game, then maybe by engaging with a developer, they can make their opinions known. This, then, becomes another mitigating factor that game developers are expected to deal with in terms of passion play: can you maintain your love of the medium, can you stomach crunch and compartmentalize it as an object of valor, and now, can you provide customer service for angry fans as well? One event that sticks in my own memory is what happened to Jessica Price, formerly of ArenaNet (*Guild Wars*, *Guild Wars 2*). Price, a well-known woman developer, was targeted by people who played *Guild Wars 2* in an attempt to "share" their opinion on how the game should be constructed/fixed. Figure 5.1 shows how Price responded.

I am still to this day unsure how this constitutes Price attacking an entire community, as Mike O'Brien says in the forum post he made about firing Price for these interactions. Additionally, in the wake of these events, Megan Farokhmanesh of The Verge talked to other women game developers who

← **Tweet**   •••

Jessica Price
@Delafina777

Today in being a female game dev:

"Allow me--a person who does not work with you-- explain to you how you do your job."

 Deroir @DeroirGaming · 3 Jul 2018
Replying to @Delafina777

Really interesting thread to read!
However, allow me to disagree "slightly". I dont believe the issue lies in the MMORPG genre itself (as your wording seemingly suggest). I believe the issue lies in the contraints of the Living Story's narrative design; (1 of 3)

5:59 pm · 4 Jul 2018 · Twitter Web Client

Figure 5.1. Jessica Price, a former ArenaNet employee, responds to criticism of her work on Guild Wars II on Twitter. *@Delafina777 on Twitter. Screenshot captured by author.*

became targets of hate campaigns trying to get them fired for their social media presence. Farokhmanesh's article "ArenaNet Firings Cast a Chilling Shadow Across the Game Industry" (2018) mentions other high-profile developers such as Jennifer Scheurle's own experience with Twitter users brigading her employer about her social media presence, citing how she does not take on criticism well and that she is not always nice to people who attack her.

The unfortunate truth of post-Gamer Gate social media is that, in concentrated groups, disgruntled gamers wield a staggering amount of power, especially if they brigade one or two individual developers. In Price's case, this series of events became a passion-measuring contest where, even though Price had worked on *Guild Wars 2* for years at this point, her passion (and pride in her work) was somehow worth less than a random streamer on Twitter. Of course, this is just one of many examples where game devs' passion for their work, and their passion for protecting what they have invested their heart and soul into, has been misconstrued by people on social media to mean that they hate the fans who play their games, and they do not think that the fans should have opinions on the games. So in addition to having to crunch to finish games, being graded in effect on how passionate (read: willing to work extra, unremunerated hours) they are about videogames, and how readily subjectivatable they are, game developers now must also deal with issues of collocation and parasocial relationship-building, lest they be accused of not respecting fans.

At points, this type of brigading actually forces crunch; or, rather, it forces a shift in office culture that takes the form of crunching to show that the passions in question are above questioning. If the company sees an increase in negative engagement with social media posts following an announced delay, or even following a poorly received update, how might that translate into workers being forced into a position where they have to crunch to either fix the problem, make up for lost time, or somehow sate the angry conscious of social media users by proving that workers are passionate about the game and passionate about delivering a good product with minimal interruptions? I believe that there is an element of collocation that we can find with discontent on social media and in survey materials and a redoubling (whether forced from the company or undertaken as a form of groupthink/groupaction) of efforts of workers. It seems too coincidental that events like the Price and ArenaNet problem occur, and then workers enter into periods of prolonged crunch and prolonged "good behavior" (meaning that developers' interactions with fans and consumers is either nonexistent or overly accommodating). Though, again, outside of the scope of this book, I think that there are connections to be drawn here that only further contour how the capitalist socius creates feedback loops that rely on daisy-chaining mechanics to get an idea of where and how bodies are affected.

The Short-Circuit

So how do we short-circuit these two issues? How do we go about removing an element of cruel optimism that, in the end, is not even *our own* cruel optimism? What would an ethic of production look like that is not beholden to the whims of the capitalist socius' need for constant surplus production? I want to start with the issue of cruel optimism that is not our own. If we are truly to take up a schizorevolutionary way of approaching problem-solving that short circuits the socius' dictations for bodies that are not a hindrance to the cycle of production in place, we must look outside of just the concepts of privacy and parasociality to think through the issue of cruelly optimistic collocation that feeds into perpetuating crunch. At the moment, there is a distinct lack of knowledge about what goes on behind the scenes in videogame production. The average person who plays games is not privy to what types of labor go into producing the media that they consume. Or, rather, the picture that *is* publicly painted is one of irreverence and lightheartedness. This is due in large part to what Bulut (2015) talks about in the form of the "shiny veneer of videogame production"; we do not see the sausage being cased, for lack of a better phrase. The general public knows that videogames are supposed to be fun, and we are treated to a constantly manicured image of game studios as being sites of fun: you play while you work, you create games, you are responsible for making the objects that people enjoy. This, in effect, solidifies an image of labor in games that is antithetical to what regular labor is conceived of in the form of long hours, backbreaking manual or mental labor, low remuneration, and spiritually unfulfilling work. The irony, of course, lies in the fact that games labor is no different in terms of long hours, backbreaking labor, and low remuneration. And arguably, based on what I have talked about regarding production workers being expected to become emotionally predatory since affective experiences are more readily becoming axiomatizable, the work itself is becoming spiritually unfulfilling as well.

This being said, transparency has always been a problem for games companies. From Blizzard to BioWare to Epic to Rockstar, transparency about inner-workings, workflows, contracts, labor commitments, employee support, meritocracy and promotion, and even earnings calls like those that Activision-Blizzard publishes are shrouded in gesturing language and noncommittal corporate buzzwording. Even apologies or public addresses such as Blizzard's 2020 lawsuits regarding sexual harassment of employees have created confusing and noncommittal responses from the company for issues that, for all intents and purposes, are very clear cut and the actions to solve those problems are also clear cut. I know that saying "transparency and honesty in all parts of game development are paramount to cutting down on the types of parasocial and cruelly optimistic abuse that we see of individual developers, which then circles back in itself as a way for the company to redirect energy towards more productive means (e.g. crunch to get the video-game out sooner so people stop bothering you)" is incredibly naïve given the hellscape that I've painted the capitalist socius and videogame production as. But, it still remains that that, and employee support in the form of companies taking active antibullying/antibrigading stances for their employees, is one of the most necessary institutional steps to cutting back the daisy chain of events that ends up with crunch as a way of showing those brigading that workers' passion is not questionable.

Though not necessarily time-friendly or work-friendly, communality in the form of collective action could be key in breaking down silos. Additionally, sharing successes might prove important to bolstering worker morale and slowing weeding out the lone-wolf or rogue-agent imagery in game produc-tion. No game is made successful by one person; it is always a communal effort. Even when considering game developers like Eric Barone of *Stardew Valley* fame, it is apparent that the act of creation is never a lone burden to bear. Barone was always very vocal about his partner's support both emotion-ally and financially while he workshopped, iterated on, and created *Stardew Valley*. Additionally, the early QA testers for *Stardew Valley* helped Barone to, in a roundabout way, consolidate his workflows so that he wasn't rebuilding entire sectors of the game from the ground up. In triple-A game development, the same necessity of communality holds true. And it is within this commu-nality that my first recommendation comes into play:

1a. Form a collective within a company that tracks grievances, stages pro-tests or pickets upon grievous injury, and negotiates the types of labor undertaken in projects. This includes demanding that companies protect workers online, in official forums, and in popular media.
1b. Until grievances are addressed, commit to slow work or "quiet quit-ting" practices. Strangle supply lines (for immaterial labor, those supply lines are often our bodies, minds, and affect), and commit to noncom-munication regarding blame-placing.

We are aware of institutional initiatives in videogame production that, on the surface, seek to garner public attention for being "inclusive" or "diverse." But what we rarely, if ever, see are these initiatives blossoming or working. This is why I am not recommending another initiative where workers approach bosses on an "even" playing field. Sarah Ahmed's book *On Being Included* (2012) outlines what material-discursive realities "initiatives" inhabit. Ahmed reflects on her own time being part of institutional initiatives, and the sense of overwhelming discouragement that she felt and faced when trying to action university-recommended diversity initiatives. Often times, these initiatives are not meant to actually accomplish the thing they are set out to, ostensibly, accomplish, such as Ahmed's work on a gender initiative. Since these initiatives are often underfunded and rarely, if ever, allocated with the necessary bodies capable of actioning the types of work necessary to affect change, initiatives like the ones that Ahmed outlines are more than likely doomed to fail, but meant, in the short term, to be a tick-box about addressing some sort of problem that the institution is aware it has. This is why I did not recommend another initiative: a worker-focused collective action group could, and probably would, be beholden to the same types of institutionalism as initiatives are. Meaning that, while on the surface an institution may seem happy to hear what a group like this has to recommend, those recommendations fall on stone deaf ears. This, then, raises the question of where can information be made public that will keep both the company and potential parasocial problematics accountable? How could a collective handle internal and external abuse?

In the most simple terms, using the capitalist socius' own systems for this measure make the most sense. Twitter and other social media platforms can act as dissemination points of what workers record in these collective action committee meetings, and they can hold bodies accountable both in-company and external to the company. Though, this then invites conversation around brigading again. Let's say that during one of these meetings, a member brings up abuse from a user on Twitter. Is it alright to record that abuser's Twitter handle in meeting notes and release their information alongside proof of their abuse? If that information is made publicly available, this begs the question of whether or not that is potential doxing or if releasing that information is in the interest of community-policing. If we are truly moving towards ushering in the processual assemblage, though, then we need to start preparing for postindividualism. At some point, this means holding accountable the individual that is potentially threatening homeostasis. I think that, in terms of co-opting the socius' tools against it and turning the subjectivatable mores of communication into schizorevolutionary interventions, making public acts of violence against community members is the first step in the correct direction of creating cohesive, ethic-of-care communities that seek to actively protect their own and encourage community growth.

A collective like this could be *akin* to a union, but more embodied and granular than an entire union structure. Whereas unions need to contend with multiple different bodies across multiple different avenues of labor, a collective embedded within a company need only contend with immediate assemblies. One of the main differences here being the aspect of "uselessness" or planned unworking. Minor subterfuge, very akin to the US's World War II tactics entitled "Simple Sabotage," would function ideally in a collective setting simply because of what Joshua Morrison in *Revelling in Uselessness: Queer and Trans Media, Consumptive Labor, and Cultural Capital* (2019) talks about with symbolic versus economic violence:

> for Bourdieu, capitalism's symbolic violence is more insidious than the physical violence of the factory that Marx fixates on because it is never recognized as a form of violence that must also be resisted if any kind of revolutionary social change is to take hold. Symbolic violence kills the will to rebel against the capitalist's exploitation of his workers before it forms. Therefore, the (re)production of dominant cultural capital is equally connected to affect, violence, hope, pain, and fear as economic capital. (43)

Within collectives, discrete milieus can be established that actively take in, reimagine, and return these symbolic violences that are wantonly inflicted on workers' bodies. When passion (and the removal of a person from their collocation with their object of desire) is invoked in the name of trying to coerce a worker to work harder or longer for no more remuneration, that is symbolic violence. Singularly, symbolic violence is a powerful subjectivation tool *because* of how subjectivation and individualism function and embed within the capitalist socius. But herein lies the power of a collective, and what we can begin to see as a preprocessual assemblage formation: symbolic violence functions well on an individual basis. But when you have a *constellation* of individuals as Guattari eludes to, the violence is then mitigated and redistributed. And in the same way that the capitalist socius strips the rights to live from nonproductive bodies, collectives have the potential of grinding the pace of a project to a halt if needs are not being met. Clumsy data storage, mishandling equipment, needing continual guidance on details or asks, recreating or overwriting models. All mistakes that happen, and all mistakes that, done systematically and over the course of days, weeks, or even months, can ultimately force negotiation on a more granular scale than a union would be capable of.

There are, of course, considerations to make regarding this. A collective like this requires all parties be in similar collocative spaces in terms of what goals they are seeking to accomplish. Akin to the processual assemblage, personalities may crop up, negative feelings, infighting, etc. but the important piece to keep in mind is that the bodies assembled in that assemblage are interested in pursuing a common subjectivational goal. This includes committing to the types of subterfuge and sabotage that I have outlined. That being said, if a body, or multiple bodies, decide to flee this protoprocessual assemblage, the bodies left in the assemblage need to be aware that, since they are still operating within the capitalist socius, retaliation is likely to occur, with little recourse. Since this *is* protoprocessual, there may not be the influx of new bodies to this processual assemblage to fill out the spaces and contours that bodies moving to other processual assemblages leaves. There also might not be other processual assemblages that, while not similar in aim, would still be there to support this processual assemblage. All of this means that, if a collective is to occur within a game company, it runs the risk of being quashed, but could also single-handedly change the culture of the company.

Unions: Cohesion across Games?

I find myself, once again, trying to tackle a behemoth of a question; on the scale of me being a tardigrade and this question being the size of a humpback whale. I want to return for a moment to work from my informants regarding what unions are, if they are important, and who they think can actually *be* in unions. 29 out of the 52 people who I have spent time with talked about unions and collective action unprompted. Opinions ranged from frustration, misunderstanding, and mistrust all the way up to unabashed support. Another 19 talked at length about unions and collective actions once I asked them what their opinions, interactions, and/or experiences were. The six informants comfortable being spot lit all brought up unionization at some point during our conversations and their specific, embodied experiences provide a good contouring for the scope of the issues at play with unions and collective action cohesion. These folks' opinions and experiences with unions ranged from being indifferent or neutral to being actively involved in fighting for collective action and trying to assist workplaces in taking formative steps towards unionization. When my informants spoke about unions, they tended to do so in context of other themes. For example, Malique talked about his experience working 80-hour weeks for 3 months on a popular online title that launched in 2016 and how the overwork ended up giving him chronic stomach ulcers. Shortly after wrapping this project and seeking medical attention, he was approached by a co-worker asking how he felt about unions. Malique said that he hadn't really given unions too much thought outside of what he had seen on Twitter or via International Game Developers Association forums/Facebook. The conversation that Malique and I had about unions was less them taking an affirmative stance and more about him using our conversation as a sounding board for how he understood current union rhetorics.

Lauren talked about unions in terms of workplace culture. She experienced a lot of negativity from her manager that manifested in abusive workplace practices. She described the experience as "the old saying 'dad yells at mom, mom yells at the kid, the kid kicks the dog, who does the dog bite? The other dog.'" Meaning that, as negativity pervaded the workplace and trickled down from management to workers, workers started to become toxic to one another because they had no outlet for the toxicity they were dealing with from management. Lauren's fellow worker's spouse brought up Game Workers Unite (GWU) to their spouse, who got in contact with GWU regarding what a union might mean in terms of making their workplace less toxic and dealing with bad management. They then brought that information to Lauren, and they worked to set up precedents to unionize their workplace. Though the original employee who brought GWU up to my informant was fired (as a note, my informant is convinced it was about trying to unionize while the reason given was "poor workplace fit"), Lauren is still carrying on trying to unionize, and has branched out to helping other game companies start unionization proceedings or figure out if unionization is the correct fit for their workplace.

Lauren and Malique's experiences serve as a reminder that this issue is not as important to everyone in videogame production as it is to a few. They also spoke about the importance of representation within media that sought to unionize people. I want to further highlight Malique and Lauren's comments as well as add in Maria's comments. Parts of my conversation with these informants presented contours regarding understanding *what* a union is, who can be part of unions, and what a union looks like from a manager's perspective. Malique, especially, brought up some important points about their experience with unions.

> We looked through [Game Worker's Unite's] twitter, and it seemed like, from their beginning, they were retweeting good stuff! But we didn't see them retweeting anyone that looked like us. Like, I think the only person of color that got retweeted was Austin Walker? It's cool that Anna [Anthropy] got retweeted, and some women got retweeted. Oh! And then we looked at their website, and I get that most of the "About" stuff is going to be slightly nebulous for something like this, but some of the answers from the FAQ they had were weird. Like, who can be in a union. The answer to that question on their website was literally anyone who does anything with games. That's good, don't get me wrong, but that, taken with who they're retweeting just didn't instill a lot of trust in me.

That Malique did not see people who looked like him being given attention via the official Twitter account of GWU *is* important to consider. It begs investigation into how, structurally, organizations that are concerned with anticapitalist practices, promoting diversity, and creating equitable working conditions mimics how the systems they are critiquing are set up. This also speaks to problem of heterogeneity within videogame production that I have brought up prior. Due to the gender imbalance within videogame production, it would follow that even countercapitalist measures within videogame production would see similar gender imbalances. Malique's comments about not seeing anyone represented that looked like him, and the language being used to describe what the official function of GWU is as "nebulous" both present important distinctions in terms of the early 2020 announcement by the Communication Workers of America (CWA) to assist videogame production workers in unionization. The CWA's official statement shares similar nebulous, nonspecific, noncommittal language with GWU's general "about" section, which signals a problem that is broader than just who we see being retweeted or shared by social media accounts. It signals a problem of scope. In the case of unionizing videogame production, the problem of an unidentified scope. There are not solid bifurcations as to who can and cannot participate in union efforts and receive union support, so we continue to see the language around unionization efforts as unwieldy and too broad.

Maria discussed concerns of theirs around who they can and cannot see being in unions that echoed the problems that Malique raised. Maria was not adamantly for or against unions, and their scrutiny of what unions meant not only for them, but for the whole of videogame production presents an important reminder about where we put emphasis in our pursuit of solving problems.

Maria: Ok, so, unions. I know what they're for. I know what the reason is. Better work conditions, less crunch, better pay, job security. Right? [I nod] Ok. So . . . who is that for? Who gets that and who doesn't?

Joshua: Ummm . . . well, according to Game Workers Unite, I think they think that *everyone* who works in videogames could get access to union help.

Maria: Ok, that's helpful. But how far reaching is that? Who are we defining as "works in videogames"? Does office staff or administrative staff get access to the union and protections? Hackers? Modders?

Joshua: Uh . . . um. I don't . . . know. Do you have any ideas regarding that?

Maria: Initially, maybe. When you think about it, everyone who has a hand in actually creating the game should definitely be included. So programmers, artists, Foley, writers, directors. But from there, for me, it becomes harder to pinpoint. I don't think, right now, there is enough of an understanding of who actually *works in videogames* to provide an objectively *correct* answer. A-and don't get me wrong, I'm not trying to mine for an objectively correct answer, but it bothers me that I can't have more clarity for myself on who my colleagues and peers might be in a union, you know? [. . .] My way of thinking, it might come down to someone who makes *money* working on videogames. But even then, y'know, I think of the Bethesda store and their half-assed attempt at monetizing mods. Are those people entitled to join the same union as someone who, say, works on *The Elder Scrolls 5 For Samsung Smart TV*? [laughs] Or do they have to make their own union? [. . .] Also, what happens to contract people? Do you think they get to be part of a union? But if *they* can be part of a union, why even bother having contract workers in the first place? If unions are fighting for job stability, and allowing people to not have to labor and overwork through contracts trying to get hired? Does that mean that the industry would shrink? I mean, if you take on a bunch of full-time people and can't really fire them, what else *would* happen, right? If that happened, then maybe the industry would stop wasting money and being so poorly managed, but I don't think that would happen in a day, you know? What seems like would come first is definitely a recession.

For Maria, the nebulous language that is associated with unionizing became a point of contention for them. Maria pointed to multiple tweets and portions of GWU's website that provided very little context about anything that GWU was about or supported. I refer back to my previous example of GWU's FAQ section that says "if you are doing any kind of job for a game company—whether that be in-house, in an agency, on contract or casual—you're a game worker." Without any sort of specificity to what issues GWU is aiming to tackle, focused plans of attack become highly improbably, and any plan that wishes to take on *all* the issues being listed is setting itself up for failure. Issues gestured toward through the website are poor pay, politics, abuse, bully/harassment, neoliberal "do what you love" mentality, overly competitive job market, crunch, weak negotiations with potential employers re: overly competitive job market, sacrificing person time in service of production. Throughout our conversation, Maria had been careful to say that they were still learning about unions, and what the unionization process could be like, but that the resources that they had at their disposal (e.g., GWU's website, Twitter, Googling "what is a union") raised more questions than they answered. Even though they had their own initial formulations about who feasibly *could* be involved with unionization and seek protection through unions, Maria's ideas about who could be protected ended up relying on the flow of capital through the institution of videogame production. Without considering how capital flows, who enables it to flow, and the real possibility of contractions in videogame production due to unionization, coming to any sort of initial understanding of who can and cannot take part in unions in production will stay abstracted and we will continue to see vague language like that from CWA and GWU.

Even though terminology around unionization is still nebulous and imprecise, Lauren talked at length not about the broad view of unionizing the videogame industry, but their own individual motivation for wanting to help unionize. Lauren's experience with organizing unionization efforts came from working crunch, and her concern with people she knew having access to working conditions that allowed them to have a normal work-life balance.

Joshua: Do you think that that stress and that separation played a part in why you gravitated towards unionization and helping with unionization so much?

Lauren: I certainly think that was part of it. I am a person who doesn't enjoy seeing other people suffer. I don't like seeing my friends, coworkers, strangers on the street sad. I think that my involvement with unions started to present these really great opportunities to not be alone in that I am always *with* people, talking about this stuff, and I am also helping people to craft plans on how *they* can get back to their families or have some sort of work-life balance that they maybe didn't have previously. I certainly think that that was part of it. [. . .] The more I worked, the more I *didn't* want to work. It was always crunch that made me fall more and more out of love. I just didn't have the passion to stay long nights or work all week anymore because I had seen a better side of things. I saw what it *could* be.

Joshua: With collective bargaining?

Lauren: That and unionization. Around the time that my contact told me about that union group, I started thinking about how I could help. How could I be productive with this.

In other parts of our conversation, Lauren said that her experience with unionizing and helping to establish union plans for videogame production companies was not done to help or hinder agencies like GWU. Lauren brought up the nebulous language on GWU's website as a point of contention for her as well when I asked. She said that, due to this, and due to her own upbringing in a primarily blue-collar household, she understood unions to be not an ideal that is intellectualized and turned over and over, but as an action plan to help people. She said that her approach in talking about unions both to people like me and to potential clients wasn't to get them to think about the whole of unionizing videogame production, but how Lauren's experiences could help potential clients to recontextualize their relationship with production to recapture a work-life balance.

While each informant had their own understanding of, contextual examples of, and interactions with unionization/the idea of unions within videogame production that ranged from indifferent to zealous, informants brought up important questions *about* unionization that, without their embodied experiences, I would not have been able to consider. What is especially important about what they shared is the attention that needs to be paid to the types of language that are currently being used to talk about unionization and what deeper issues this signals. The problems that my informants identified characterize a fundamental misunderstanding, or possibly a fundamental *refusal* to understand, what constitutes precarity within videogame production on the part of union outfits.

A recent example of this lack of understanding comes from the CWA's announcement in January of 2020 that they would be assisting tech and videogame production workers in unionization efforts. For such a large unionization body to step forward and announce that they would be deploying resources *specifically* to help game workers unionize is exciting news. But the CWA's statement repeats many of the same problems that other unionization outfits like GWU cannot seem to move past, and raises new concerns as well. The CWA seems to be linking tech workers and game workers together, without any sort of distinction between the two, or who is eligible for this new initiative. Game workers and tech workers are used interchangeably both in the official statement put forth by CWA president Chris Shelton and on the initiative's website. There is also a distinct lack of actionable plans put forth. In the statement released by Shelton, more time is spent discussing who the initiative has hired and their merits than what the actual problems being addressed are. Similarly, on the Campaign to Organize Digital Employees (CODE-CWA)'s website, there is a lack of any sort of plans of action, previous research, acknowledgment of specific cases where actions listed in Shelton's press release have occurred, or ways in the interim to help to start to talk to coworkers about organizing. Instead, there are buzzwords that adorn the front page, a very stark summary of "rights," and an "about" section that does nothing to characterize the immediate, timely actions being taken by the initiative (if any).

Without any sort of plan in place, or a plan even hinted at, my informants' concerns are substantiated. The CWA, CODE, and GWU are not *not* equipped to make inroads. There is capital behind these groups, there are people willing to collectivize, but there is a distinct lack of current videogame production workers' voices being heard or acknowledged. Within that lack of acknowledgment, the "issues" that CWA, CODE, and GWU discuss are void of any meaningful engagement. For *whom* are these situations precarious? Every single videogame production worker? Marginal workers? Only certain, nonquantifiable people? As it stands, the issues that the CWA identifies in their statement are all just blanketly "bad" and need to be "fixed" without any deeper engagement with those issues or the circumstances that have *caused* those issues. As my informants have stated, the media presence of very well-known videogame production unionization groups tells them nothing about what the initiative does or is advocating for and does nothing to acknowledge in substantial ways the types of precarity that videogame production workers face. As Malique stated about their experience with unionization in videogame production, "Nothing is a one-size-fits-all solution." In addition to this, these union outfits are not acknowledging any understanding of the contours of the precarities within videogame production. Issues such as overwork are gestured towards, but there is no contextualization done, nor are there any ethnographic accounts being given. *Why* are workers overworking? What is causing workers to be ok with overwork? Who is dictating that they must overwork? Until unionization outfits put forth understandings around contributing factors to precarities, different forms of precarities that different workers face, and also acknowledge that precarities do not manifest the same for every production worker, unionization will continue to be a hollow, well-meaning activity that, akin to cupcake fascism, diverts energy away from rooting the cause of the problem in favor of feeling good about taking a stand against the problem.

AN ALTERNATIVE TO UNIONS?

I will preface this section by saying that I do not think that there is an easy, ready-made alternative to unionization in any form, but especially in videogame production. Unions like we see in material labor become incredibly difficult to reproduce or find alternatives to simply because of how immaterial labor works. Unions, especially when we think of the power of unions in pre-Thatcher Britain, present such powerful vehicles of equalization for workers that it becomes difficult to think of something better that is actually actionable today, as is our goal. By virtue of doing labor that does not required embodied, on-site presence, we open ourselves up to precarities in the form of misattribution, de- and reclassification, and a much looser definition of what, where, and how work is being remunerated. The simplest example is the concept of clocking in and out. In material labor, there are expectations that bodies are on-site, performing labor for a certain number of hours. That labor usually cannot be taken home or performed offsite simply because of the need for machinery, architecture, and specific environments. For example, if I worked at a car manufacturing plant, I might be expected to work 10 hours, 4 days a week. I would clock in at a certain time, work on whatever part of the assembly line that I was assigned to, and then clock off. The expectation around that type of labor and remuneration structure is very clear.

With immaterial labor, the abstraction of organic bodies from inorganic bodies makes the work less, well, material. When considering videogame production, most types of labor associated with making a game are immaterial: sound design, coding, modeling and rigging, corporate communication, community management, etc. This was made especially clear during the COVID pandemic. Bungie, for example, went to great lengths to outline how they were employing a working from home model while still committing to a full release schedule for *Destiny 2*, which included a YouTube video[2] that outlined expectations for workers and what fans could expect. But even prior to the

COVID pandemic and the proliferation of remote work, immaterial labor in videogame production only required things like mixing equipment for sound and voice recording; computers and development consoles capable of running asset-creation software, compiling the games, and playing builds; some desk space; and some meeting space. The most important aspects of videogame production work are, akin to material labor, the specialized apparatuses that are required to do certain types of labor. But, unlike the specialized apparatuses of material labor, the apparatuses needed for videogame production are almost ubiquitous to the common tech worker's home: a computer, a workspace, and internet connection. There are various other accessories that are role-dependent like, again, sound mixing equipment, or drawing tablets, but the necessity for highly specialized, highly architecturalized machinery just is not there in a way that would prevent working comfortable from a variety of spaces that are not offices.

If we return to our definition of the processual assemblage as something that is uniquely postindividualistic and something that propagates and creates new agencements in the form of autopoietic nuclei, then what *might* an alternative to unions, or even a modification of unions, look like for videogame production? Something that accounts for the unique challenges of attribution, specificity, and immaterial work? Again, too, we must invoke *amor implicationis* as a reminder of how ontoethics focuses on contours of entanglement if we are trying to think outside of what a normal union might look like. We triangulated passion, cruel optimism, and precarities all as attributions and enablers for the way that videogame production subjectivates bodies. However, the discussion around cruel optimism and passion only evolved far enough to allow for contouring to happen around negative aspects, and it only evolved enough to highlight them as potential policing mechanism. Instead, let us reimagine what passion and cruel optimism operate as. Again, referring back to the processual assemblage's place within the forthcoming ethicoaesthetic socius, passion could go from a policing measure to the nuclei that O'Sullivan (2010) talks about. Passion can be the thing continually folding in upon itself and reconfiguring itself. Passion as the nuclei would act similarly to autopoiesis as it is presently thought of in the capitalist socius in that there would be libidinal energies continually occupying the BwO with new becomings and new agencements. However, in the ethicoaesthetic socius, it would be vastly different in that those energies are not serving to prop up a production method, and they do not require strict and machinic regulations, nor do they require specific and stringent subjectivation to function. In fact, those energies and becomings spill over and out of each assemblage where a nuclei is housed; they cross-pollinate with other assemblages. The overspill and what would formerly be value surplus of labor can permutate and create new assemblages with different shades, shapes, and flavors of passion within videogame production. This could mean that new types of games are created, or new workflows are created. This could even mean that we recondition ourselves as to what videogames creation even is! But this nucleic information becomes a swirling, growing, breathing mass in the processual assemblage whereas now, it is simply a culture policing measure, meant to weed out bodies whose passion is not subjectivated to the form-fit that the socius requires for smooth production.

Similarly to our passion-nuclei, cruel optimism must also find new life. Herein lies an important semantic shift from Berlant's *cruel* optimism. Her work, and my work, have only really collocated bodies in proximity to objects that they need to function, or to objects that, without proximity to, their agency is threatened. The way that cruel optimism could work in this new process would be by changing the object of attachment. Part of creating a postindividualist assemblage is moving past neoliberal ideations of what constitutes identity, what constitutes community, and what constitutes our entanglements in the two. This would mean almost circling back to the savage socius in terms of organization around objects and concepts; we collocate ourselves with like-minded people, and we collocate ourselves to people with similar ethics: ethics of care, ethics of slowness, ethics of love, ethics of entanglement variance. Again, invoking that Butlerian and Hardt-and-Negrian concept of "assembly." Ultimately, we are seeking to collocate ourselves with other productive bodies, creating an object. The postindividual aspect of this collocation, though, is that we would be combining passions. These assemblages, where our passion-nuclei is constantly rebecoming, require cohesive, ethic-driven, and nondeterministic cohesion of bodies to contour what the agencements that are present within that assemblage. Therefore, the "cruel" part of "cruel optimism" becomes less cruel; it goes from a potentially cruel collocation activity to one where collocation equates to productivity and freedom.

I know what you are thinking. The renegotiation of the two elements I have just done sounds suspiciously like forming communes or suggesting that videogame production needs to take on aspects of communism. In short, no. Communism, and communes in general, rely on the idea of equal distribution of services, goods, and power. But inevitably, there is a breakdown in structure because of how flat the hierarchy is. The human condition is not one of mutual assurance or uniformity, and ultimately communism requires uniformity in ideas, goals, and drive in order to function. Instead, I am gesturing towards a reconfiguration of our entanglements by way of using the capitalist socius' tools against it. Therefore, I have a two-part (technically three-part) recommendation:

1a: Nurture more initiatives shaped like Pixelles and Dames Making Games. Nurture initiatives where members have similar goals, similar passions, similar ethics, and similar ideology. Creating something akin to, or in the spirit of, the ethicoaesthetic socius within videogame production will elevate the need for communal, ethical care of our passions, ideas, and each other.

1b: It will also elevate the need for guarding our resources (passion, energy, understanding, etc.) and making sure that we are sharing those resources with those that will be energized by them, and who, in turn, will energize us. This can only be done when we surround ourselves with people whose passions and intentions complement our own, and we are pursuing work that fulfills all parties. This also means developing the fortitude and affective resilience necessary to understand when we outgrow an assemblage, or another body outgrows our assemblage, and seek new entanglements. Additionally, it means being thankful for the entanglements we have from moment-to-moment, year-to-year, and lifetime-to-lifetime regardless of where our next step leads us, or what it may lead us away from.

2: Divest from structures that require continually reproving your passions and requiring that your passion be collocated alongside a means of production. This does not mean quit your job or quit striving to make it in/into videogame production. Instead, it means reassess what energy you give to corporate videogame development and the subjectivation required of you.

These recommendations are obviously easier said than done, as is the case with my first recommendation. But, as I said previously, examples of this type already exist. Even though they do not necessarily supplant the need for unions, or the services that a union provides, they do provide a sort of shelter that unions cannot provide. They provide spaces where your passion can shift and grow alongside others, but can still be challenged in respectful ways.

One problem, of course, with these types of initiatives is funding. Unfortunately, we still do have to operate within the constraints of the capitalist socius, which means that, at some point, capital is going to be an issue unless these initiatives are grassroots, DIY ventures from start to finish. They may start as that, but eventually, given proper time and nurturing, they will most likely outgrow DIY spaces. Now, some countries provide grants or assistance to offset some of the costs of running initiatives like this (specific to Pixelles and Dames Making Games, that country is Canada), but grant funding for the arts is increasingly eroding across most of the western world. Additionally, these types of initiatives must contend with being grouped into the same arenas as things like ReFiG. ReFiG was a Canadian grant-funded initiative that invited games scholars, game creators, and game culture enthusiasts across the world to apply for grant funding packages to carry out books. I want to say that I am intensely grateful for the hospitality, networking, and idea generation that I was a part of with most of the people I interacted with in ReFiG. I also want to thank the earnest members of their steering committee such as Dr. Nicholas Taylor and Dr. Sarah Evans. While most elements of ReFig were earnest, and the work done by participants, grant-holders, and the communities that sprung up around them was positive, the co-PIs of the project came under scrutiny for transphobic remarks and actions in addition to decades of labor exploitation that reached far outside of just this project. Instead of apologizing and attempting to amend their mistakes, they doubled down and made a research presentation at AIOR in 2020 titled "Twittering Research, Calling Out and Canceling Cultures: A Story and Some Questions." I refuse to cite their work, nor give power to names as destructive as theirs are. Suffice it to say that, as the funding pool gets muddied with "initiatives" such as this that end up showcasing how destructive falling into the trap of replicating institutional power can be, the initiatives that actually do fight for and espouse positive values will suffer due to name- and subject-association.

The other glaring problem is that these initiatives do not provide the legal, monetary protections that a union does. Again, unions as a construct for worker protection present almost incomparable benefits given the material-discursive circumstances we find ourselves imbricated in in the capitalist socius. Almost to the point that it genuinely becomes difficult not to just continue pushing for the full unionization of videogame production at all levels, across all affiliations, and across all types of labor while saying "damn the semantics." But, again, this is not a readily executable ontoethical intervention. So much more work is required *around* the semantics of who, what, when, where, and how that it is not in any way fair to do anything more than simply try and provide the first steps and gestures towards that work, alongside a groundwork around passion and precarities. Additionally, it only seems fair to try to provide alternatives that align with our definition of ontoethics that we can go out and start cultivating immediately.

Again, though, in the sense of using the capitalist socius' own tools against itself, these recommendations, and these reconfigurations of passion and cruel optimism provide ground on which we can start to chip away at the socius' subjectivational hold on videogame production. These are not perfect methods, and there has been, I fear, too little consideration given to the granular and embodied insofar as how these recommendations actually may play out, if they may play out at all. I know that these recommendations, too, are asking already tired workers to take on additional taxing activities in order to try and begin fixing what is broken and begin forging a new path. But, the hope that I feel wrapped up in these recommendations came from sources that we can gesture towards and actively observe today! There are always glimmers of hope within videogame production, and that is incredibly important to remember when doing this type of work. But without performing the labor to spread that hope, we will find ourselves mired time and time again in the same types of bastardization of former glimmers of hope. Things like triple-A studios creating affectively driven personal games to prey on the art form's rise to prominence in queer and alternative game making communities. We risk always falling back into tired ways as soon as complacency starts to ingrain itself in rising anticapitalist creation methods. Additionally, we always have to stay wary of the ways in which the capitalist socius is reconfiguring itself and its autopoietic subjectivation cycles to begin extracting capital out of anti-capital-generating methodologies.

ARE "RECOMMENDATIONS" ENOUGH?
IN SHORT, NO. IN LONG, NOOO.

I readily admit that the recommendations that I have laid out in this chapter are idealistic to say the *very* least. I also readily admit that there are holes in consideration that I cannot, in the scope of just this book, correct. For example, would it not have made more sense to interview CWA and GWU organizers and include them as part and parcel of my informants' conception? Yes, it would have been. And I did partially do that labor. I interviewed three CWA workers familiar with the work being done on videogame production unionization, and their conception of what was going on with that was vastly different than the types of labor, passion, precarities, workflows, becomings, and intensities I have already spoken about. Not different in a negative way, however; different in a way that approaches unionization from an institutional, industrial level as opposed to a granular, embodied level. While my work may present a rough estimation of the molecular quandaries present in videogame production, these workers' conceptions present the macro view which requires a completely different tool kit to approach and break down. One that requires negotiations of institutional ontonlogies, feminist post-Marxism, Neotaylorism and Neofordism, political theory, a reconnection and recontextualization of Munozian queer utopics, a reapproach to queerness and failure a la Halberstam. In other words, approaching considerations of what is and is not happening in terms of speaking to the people who have stated they have an institutional, corporate, vested interest in unionization and collective action within videogame production requires a completely renewed and recontextualized approach. This is simply because of the institutional rhetoric that the bodies imbricated with unionizing tech workers in the US use and their cruelly optimistic collocation (or lack thereof) to objects of attachment.

So while those embodied, experiential accounts of CWA and GWU work-ers *are* incredibly important for painting a fuller, more robust picture of the landscape we are all imbricated in, the semiotic, ontological approaches are impossibly different and require their own diligence.

And herein, I think, lies the problem with "recommendations." The recom-mendations I am making in this book are being made based on very specific theoretical turns and very specific, embodied knowledge. They require uncomfortably similar situationality to what Weber characterizes ideal types as. The types of bodies who can undertake these recommendations are truly exceptional bodies and they inhabit exceptional spaces. By virtue of the argu-ments I have made around passion and precarities, especially, it should be apparent that not everyone can afford to undertake these recommendations in their current form. This, again, falls to the discussion around in-betweeners. To what extent are we *safe* to undertake these recommendations? However, there is no truly safe step towards ushering in the processual assemblage, nor is there a safe way of ushering in new ethicoaesthetics for videogame production. There is, as with my conception of precarities, always risk. Each action we undertake in trying to set ourselves in closer collocation to a (pre) processual assemblage has associated risk that is part and parcel of existing in the capitalist socius and existing in the hostile-to-life environs of late-stage capitalism. I think the practicalities that I have addressed in this chapter are somewhat more tempered than the extents that I could have gone to by invok-ing Deleuze and Guattari, O'Sullivan and Grosz, Berlant and Ngai. But I want to avoid the idealism that these type of scholarly-activism can fall into. Videogame production and the capitalist socius have not gotten where they are today by being easily penetrable or having vast open slits in autopoietic armor. Hence, these recommendations, though formative, may still feel scant in terms of the radical theory that I have evoked. However, these feelings I have of inadequacy and scantness I recognize as part of my own *amor impli-cationis*. I fully embrace that not everyone will agree with the lengths (or shorts) that I've drawn these recommendations, nor will everyone agree with my logic about *why* I might have stopped short. That only means that there is, obviously, more work to be done, more writing to be done, more embedding and interviewing and interacting and picketing and protesting and radicaliz-ing to be done. My own entanglement with these issues will not end until the issues end, and for that, I am incredibly excited.

NOTES

1. This is in reference to a suite that a senior *World of Warcraft* developer named Alex Afrasiabi established at BlizzCon (Blizzard's yearly conference about its

games/culture/etc.). The suite, named The Cosby Suite, was filled with alcohol and as seen in texts and Facebook posts of Afrasiabi's, had the intent of being used as a hook-up/"networking" spot and not as anything to do with rape/exploitation, even though rape allegations for Cosby had been swirling at the time.

2. Bungie—Working from Home 2020—YouTube (https://www.youtube.com/watch?v=ENNWGpvoIxY)

Conclusion

It's All Over but the Crying

I want to end this book by going over two subjects that I have covered to some degree, but I feel like do not quite have a place in this work, or need some more thought put to them that is not quite as mired in theory. The first is unions and collective action, and the second is diversity, gender renegotiation, and "initiatives." I made mention of wanting to create the groundwork for more intensive work on the semantics surrounding who, what, when, where, and how unionization and collective action can take place, and I think that that requires a deeper dive into some tangential areas of digital media where unionization *is* happening. It also requires some retrodding of ground that I have already covered, but done in more industry-focused, example-driven ways.

In much the same way, I want to think through something that, historically, has been leveraged as a way of eliding talk about unions or collective action, and that is workplace initiatives around diversity, workplace culture, and gender. Diversity initiatives, according to Sara Ahmed in *On Being Included* (2012) talks about the institutional circuitry at work within "initiatives." Ahmed says that too often, diversity initiatives are understaffed, underfunded, and underscrutinized because the point of those initiatives is not to succeed, but instead to be a checkbox that the institution can gesture towards when asked. Often times, too, initiatives are foisted upon bodies of color, women, and queer bodies in an attempt to be "more diverse" and "more inclusive" when in actuality the labor being foisted is not in lieu of their other work, but in addition to it, and without remuneration or support. That is one reason I was hesitant to suggest worker-led committees as a possible ontoethical intervention since I know from experience the types of affective tolls that labor similar to initiatives can take, and could possible come across as needing to succeed.

The hope for this conclusion is that, by examining these issues given the theoretical diligence I have committed to, I *can* actually produce groundwork upon which we can start to build the semantic frameworks necessary to start actually characterizing what unions in videogame production could look like. It is no small task, but then again, this work has been "no small task." The importance of these issues, and the importance of what I have spent this text outlining are not small, either, though.

THOUGHTS ON US UNIONS (OR LACK THEREOF) AND THE PART OF IMMATERIAL LABOR

When considering unions and collective action in videogame production, there is still a sizable hole in how we talk about unions. This is due to immaterial labor and knowledge-production jobs in a digital age presenting distinct differences from any type of job before. Due to the interconnectedness that the internet provides, immaterial labor and knowledge-production jobs are no longer tied to a physical location insofar as they require resources in physical locations to do the work. Software programmers, for example, do not necessarily have to be in the office to write code. Nor does a community manager have to be in the office to interact with the community they manage. A staff writer for a digital news outlet has unprecedented hypermobility when compared to journalists in the past. Due to these new material discursive conditions of work, conditions of exploitation are different, which means that conditions under which collective action can happen effectively are different. New strategies need to be developed to put comparable pressure on management that, say, a walk-out or a picket line would do for material laborers. While collective action strategies such as walkouts and picketing can still be used to signpost the need for change and can be used to make a point about working concerns (see: Riot employee walk-out over company's toxic culture in 2019[1] or the three walkouts from Blizzard employees from 2021 to 2022 over Ravens Software layoffs, sexual abuse allegations, and vaccine requirements for workers being dropped),[2] they lack the ability to stop the flow of money as effectively as these strategies do in material labor. For example, in 2018, half of Eugen Systems, a French videogame production company, staged a walk-out that turned into a strike to protest Eugen System's blatant violation of labor laws. The strike lasted from February of 2018 until April, when strikers gave up due to lack of progress. In an update to this case, Travailleurs et Travailleuses du Jeu Vidéo (The Video Game Workers Union of France), posted a press release in late December detailing how 6 of the 21 workers involved in the labor dispute had been fired by Eugen Systems for "negatively affecting the mood of the studio." Unbeknownst to strikers,

Eugen Systems pressured nonstriking workers into crunching, and outsourced work to a now-defunct asset firm in Malaysia.

Fernandez and Fisher in "More than 30 Media Companies Have Unionized in the Past 2 Years" say that almost every "digital media" company that comes up in conversations regarding unionization is a news outlet. Why is it that news outlets have such seemingly good success as opposed to software production companies? Or videogame production? Or TV production? In large part, this is due to the structural unionization that occurred with the American Newspaper Guild (ANG) between the 1930s to 1960s. Bonnie Brennen (1996) in "Cultural Discourse of Journalists" characterizes how the ANG's unionization push was inspired by material labor unions such as mechanics, factory workers, and transport workers (84). The ANG recognized that the union structures in material labor provided a good initial model for success, but they also recognized that, to succeed in the goal of creating a collective bargaining entity that would be able to pressure management, provide workers with the same types of job safety and arbitration protection that material labor unions did, the ANG had to recontextualize who they were seeking to protect, what they were seeking to protect from, and bargaining tactics. Daniel Leab talks specifically about workday considerations that the ANG made. Before the ANG stepped in, newspaper workers had unregulated working hours, unregulated pay, and unregulated editing standards. To solve these problems, the ANG had to establish who could be considered for protection, which meant that delineations had to be made in who was and wasn't a full-fledged "journalist." Though the guidelines regarding who is a journalist and who is a contributor has shifted over the years (and has all but disappeared with digital media and online news), the general rule of thumb remained that staff writers, or those who would work 8–12 hour shifts researching, writing, fact-checking, and producing news items would be considered for ANG membership. Contingent staff that directly contributed to these jobs, but did not fall within the guidelines, could not be considered. Therefore, they became known as "contributors."

Lee Wilkins and Bonnie Brennen in "Conflicted Interests, Contested Terrain" talk about how, in a digital age, journalism has become less material, meaning that worker classifications are in flux (299). In terms of what this means for digital media and online news organizations now, we can see that there have been subtle recontextualizations, but that the basic framework of the ANG's membership understanding is still in place. Websites like BuzzFeed, HuffPost, and Vice have news journalists who are responsible for producing, editing, researching, and fact-checking work that is then distributed. In much the same way as journalists under the ANG unionized, it is mainly this rank of person across any digital media or online news organization that belong to unions. For BuzzFeed, this rank is referred to as "Buzzfeed

News Reporter." Vice refers to core writers as "Staff Writers," and advertises jobs as such, and HuffPost refers to core writers as "reporters" and advertises jobs as such.

There is, then, a rather unclear list of other classifications that fall into contingent/contributor roles, or, full-time, commensurate roles that are either excluded from unionization privileges or only given *some* protection. For BuzzFeed, for example, there are multiple "correspondent" ranks depending on the category of news you look at: investigations correspondents such as Jane Bradley or world correspondent such as Mike Giglio. Additionally, there are multiple different classifications of "staff" that are associated with writing: Farrah Penn, who is classified as a BuzzFeed Staff Writer, Kayla Yandoli, who is classified as just BuzzFeed Staff, and Laura Wright, who is classified as a BuzzFeed contributor.

There are still unanswered questions regarding best practices to unionizing and creating pressure when talking about digital media jobs. Even digital journalism, which has the most thorough and progressive union model, presents a multitude of problems regarding contingent labor, who gets counted in when talking about unions, and who/how we refer to union-eligible people. In videogame production, the same problems exists. There is a dearth of understanding of who can be in a union, who counts as contingent labor, how contingent labor is remunerated (if at all), and where/how contingent labor fits into union plans. One possible crisis that could come with unionization is that more and more of the workforce becomes contract labor. This will most likely be due to the pressure that unionizing will put on production. The current contract labor model of videogame production proves that continued emphasis on operationalizing passion and the cultural capital that working in videogames brings is enough to establish a caste of workers that will strive to break through cruel optimism. I am concerned that, as unionization starts to gain traction, and distinctions are made between who can and cannot rely on union protection, there is a lacking legal safety net that will prevent companies from firing all but essential personnel. As with any event that displaces workers and creates precarity, marginalized people will be disproportionately affected. When, not if, this occurs, then another overhaul of how we understand unions in videogame production will be necessary.

There is interest and movement towards unionization in the US, but, as my informants have said to me, that movement is mired in reticence. Each of the six informants I introduced earlier talked to me to some extent about what the purpose of unions was to them. For some, it was to create fair working conditions. For others, it was to create actionable plans towards addressing precarity. For both of these groups, though, unions represented a path forward for them to harmonize what they enjoyed about the industry with what they didn't; a middle-ground where their problems and their colleagues' problems could be solved. What my informants spoke about around unions presents important instances where the definitional work of precarity from my first chapter can be updated in respect to what these workers experience. Unionization continues to be something that videogame production workers are pushing for, but it never seems to get any closer. According to my informants, this is due in large part to the lack of a cohesive narrative, lack of actionable plans, and lack of representation. The problems that my informants identified characterize a fundamental misunderstanding, or possibly a fundamental *refusal* to understand, what constitutes precarities within videogame production on the part of union outfits.

One major example of this lack of understanding comes from the Communication Workers of America's (CWA) announcement in January of 2020 that they would be assisting tech and videogame production workers in unionization efforts. For such a large unionization body to step forward and announce that they would be deploying resources *specifically* to help game workers unionize is exciting news! But the CWA's statement repeats many of the same problems that other unionization outfits like Game Workers Unite can't seem to move past, and raises new concerns as well. The CWA seems to be linking tech workers and game workers together, without any sort of distinction between the two, or who is eligible for this new initiative. Game workers and tech workers are used interchangeably both in the official statement put forth by CWA president Chris Shelton and on the initiative's website. There is also a distinct lack of actionable plans put forth. In the statement released by Shelton, more time is spent discussing who the initiative has hired and their merits than what the actual problems being addressed are. Similarly, on the Campaign to Organize Digital Employees (CODE-CWA)'s website, there is a lack of any sort of plans of action, previous research, acknowledgment of specific cases where actions listed in Shelton's press release have occurred, or ways in the interim to help to start to talk to coworkers about organizing. Instead, there are buzzwords that adorn the front page, a very stark summary of "rights," and an "about" section that does nothing to characterize the immediate, timely actions being taken by the initiative (if any).

Union outfits like GWU say this about who would be covered by a union: "We strongly believe in the industrial model of unionization, meaning if you are doing any kind of job for a game company—whether that be in-house, in an agency, on contract, or casual—you're a game worker" (gameworkersunit. com; FAQ—"Who would be covered by a union for game workers?"). Again, the language being employed to characterize who can and cannot be included in unions and collective action is nebulous and without context. Though they recognize casual labor as a type of games work, there is no contextual information for *what types* of casual labor constitute games work. This sort of nonspecificity will continue to hamper progress towards collective action.

Without any sort of plan in place, or a plan even hinted at, my informants' concerns are substantiated. The CWA, CODE, and GWU are not *not*
equipped to make inroads. There is capital behind these groups, there are
people willing to collectivize, but there is a distinct lack of current videogame
production workers' voices being heard or acknowledged. Within that lack
of acknowledgment, the "issues" that CWA, CODE, and GWU discuss are
void of any meaningful engagement. For *whom* are these situations precarious? Every single videogame production worker? Marginal workers? Only
certain, nonquantifiable people? As it stands, the issues that the CWA identifies in their statement are all just blanketly "bad" and need to be "fixed"
without any deeper engagement with those issues or the circumstances that
have *caused* those issues. As my informants have stated, the media presence
of very well-known videogame production unionization groups tells them
nothing about what the initiative does or is advocating for and does nothing
to acknowledge in substantial ways the types of precarity that videogame
production workers face. Malique, in talking about their experience with
unionization in videogame production, said "Nothing is a one-size-fits-all
solution." In addition to this, these union outfits are not acknowledging any
understanding of the contours of precarities within videogame production.
Issues such as overwork are gestured towards, but there is no contextualization done, nor are there any ethnographic accounts being given. *Why* are
workers overworking? What is causing workers to be ok with overwork?
Who is dictating that they must overwork? Until unionization outfits put
forth understandings around contributing factors to precarity, different forms
of precarity that different workers face, and also acknowledge that precarity
does not manifest the same for every production worker, unionization will
continue to be a hollow, well-meaning activity that, akin to cupcake fascism,
diverts energy away from rooting the cause of the problem in favor of feeling
good about taking a stand against the problem.

All of this to say, there *is* a glimmer of hope for US unionization in the
form of Game Workers Alliance. Workers from Raven Software QA were
officially certified as a union on May 24, 2022, after the National Relation
and Labor Board of the United States (NRLB) certified the vote. After an
incredible stint of assault from Activision Blizzard in the form of threats to
withhold promotion and remuneration, attempted backroom dealings with
management that circumvented the workers, and emails from management
begging members not to unionize, Raven Software was able to finally ratify
their unionization to become the first official US videogame production
union. At the time of writing, no future plans have been discussed with Raven
Software about what this means for them or their workflow, what it might
mean for them to continue being housed under Activision Blizzard, or what
issues they expect to encounter in the future. I do genuinely believe that time

should be taken to bask in this victory and to examine elements of what I spoke about in the fourth chapter about the processual assemblage slowly migrating through the deterritorialized assemblage. We have been treated to examples of the capitalist socius trying to carrion-bird pieces of this concept within the third assemblage in the form of Activision Blizzard publicizing the King's Diversity Space Tool[3] in the same period as Blizzard leadership sent out active anti-union messaging. James Batchelor's whistle-blowing article "Activision Blizzard's Anti-Union Efforts Continue ahead of Raven Vote" released on May 10, while the King's Diversity Space Tool post released on May 11/12. This is quite an on-the-nose representation of how the capitalist socius has been actively sabotaged and is attempting to generate knowledge capital via a recently consumable tool: diversity. The socius will always actively struggle with subsuming and monetizing unionization since the actual point of unionization is to put stop-gaps in place for exploitation.

THOUGHTS ON DIVERSITY INITIATIVES, WORKPLACE CULTURE, AND GENDER

Thinking about diversity is impossible without thinking about institutional discourse and the circuitry that operates within organizations. We operate within late-capitalism, and companies still operate within the confines of capital. Companies must have a budget, expenses, some sort of good(s) or service(s), some manner of storefront or professional presence. Within each institution the discourses around what and who is valued affect business plans and vice-versa. Therefore, when thinking about diversity's place within institutions, it boils down to two main questions. First being "how does 'diversity' affect capital generation?" The second question stems from the first: "how can 'diversity' be given credence without ruining the subjectivation measures in place to create willingly exploitable people"? To understand how the capitalist socius is intimately tied to issues of institutional heterogeny, it is necessary to look at how subjectivation occurs within videogame production, and how that subjectivation encourages nondiversity. This, then, will leave room to discuss how diversity is "done," why it is "done" how it is, and what good, if any, that does for creating diverse places.

Capitalism is complicit in perpetuating binaries by creating and maintaining the material properties of bodily normativity by linking things such as gender to colors, masculinity or femininity to clothes and hygiene products, and masculinity/femininity to sports. It also allows rampant cultural subjectivation in other strata. For example, in the videogame production process, hypermasculinity, antifeminism, and colonialism are common storylines in videogames. But the question remains: how, and why, are these tropes perpetuated, even in games that are supposed to be progressive and inclusive?

Current videogame production processes are beginning to understand and recognize that affective and emotionally investing games can be monetized. Doris Rusch, in *Making Deep Games* and Katherine Isbister in *How Games Move Us* cover how affect can be used to create hooks in the same way that, previously, action and hyperviolence created content that appealed to certain people. So, whereas intimate, timely experiences that were rendered in videogame form used to be prevalent only in DIY and nonprofessional spaces, such as a (in)famous indie incubator called Difference Engine Initiative covered by Stephani Fisher and Alison Harvey in "Intervention for Inclusivity" (2013), the capitalist socius has begun to develop the tools to consume and repurpose these game types in service of capitalism. In professional videogame development spaces, the people creating these affective experiences and attachments have not changed; in fact, the people in these spaces have stayed much the same: white, male, and heterosexual. This has fostered an increasingly toxic and predatory work environment where videogame production workers must labor under subjectivation regimes of not only being ok with creating and perpetuating antifeminine, hypermasculine, colonialist, and antihomo/ transsexual media, but now also creating affectively and emotionally predatory media as well. This further instantiates the dehumanizing cynicism that Lazzarato talks about in "Immaterial Labor" by expecting workers to cede any moral judgment or objections to books and just get on with them.

Change in these realms does not happen with any urgency. Videogame production spaces are risk-averse and are often so locked to capitalistic production cycles that even *if* a studio wanted to rehabilitate its culture, often that cannot happen due to the nature of stagnation that the capitalist socius favors. Simply put, slow, incremental changes to videogame IPs and genres is prized over innovation and newness, both in triple-A production spaces and indie production spaces. This perspective speaks to the Guattarian notion of heterogenesis as being "an active, immanent singularization of subjectivity, as opposed to a transcendent, universalizing and reductionist homogenization . . . an expression of desire, of a becoming that is always in the process of adapting, transforming and modifying itself in relation to its environment" (*The Three Ecologies,* 95n49). Heterogeny and iterative design are locked together in videogame production because they are part and parcel of what Guattari referred to with cinema in *The Three Ecologies* (28). Like I said previously, videogame production is an enculturation endeavor and is responsible for subjectivating large sectors of the population, meaning that, as culture evolves, and as media evolves, there are certain points of entanglement where an expanding media form has the opportunity to start creating new semiotic markers and new ways of collocating with those semiotic markers.

Basically, making new types of culture. For Guattari, it was cinema. For me and us, it is videogames.

Capitalism has allowed videogame production to target certain audiences, readily subjectivate them to accept certain bodily, racial, and sexual portrayals as valid, and only those portrayals as valid. Any attempt to break with those readily recognizable tropes would mean that the entire industry would have to radically reformat not only itself, but to whom it is marketing or risk the entire medium crumbling in on itself from alienating faithful consumers. We saw the most brazen forms of hypermasculinity and hypersexualization, I would argue, in the PlayStation 1 era: games like the original three *Tomb Raiders*, though not graphically impressive like the games we have today, was marketed on pure sex appeal.[4] This sort of "valid identity" policing can, again, be seen played out in the culture of videogame production spaces. The people at work creating the subjectivizing material have themselves been subjectivized to some degree into accepting the validity of only certain people for the medium, and whether consciously or not, that subjectivization has embedded itself in workplace cultures that actively favor (mostly white) straight men for meritocratic purposes. In addition to this identity policing, there is also the rising push for videogame production to produce emotionally charged narrative work that, instead of preying on *bodily* characteristics, has started preying on affective characteristics and slice-of-life uncertainty in unfolding events. Games such as *Life Is Strange*, for example, are created by triple-A studios, and have a seemingly infinite cast of quirky, too-wise-for-their-age youths of approximately almost-adult age undertaking very specific and very emotionally driven series of events that are meant to be emotionally evocative and are meant to have wildly diverse casts because of who is being marketed to. *Life Is Strange* is a good example of how the capitalist socius has began to monetize issues like cultural, sexual, and racial diversity to try and reach new market sectors and begin the work of subjectivating new communities. While this may not seem outwardly concerning, or might in fact seem like a good thing, it needs to be considered in proximity to game studio culture as it stands.

Large developers encourage heterogeneity throughout their studios. If the production processes and workflows are similar, it is easier to identify where and when a system is breaking down so that it can be rectified. Brett Neilson and Ned Rossiter in "From Precarity to Precariousness and Back Again" talk about how nodes in a network breakdown if the structures become incongruent. This means that, as more nodes are added to a network, the structure of those networks have more edges through which non-normative productive behavior can occur, which will throw the whole network into turmoil. If the workspaces are similar, it follows that, as more heterogenic elements are incorporated into the life of a studio, even games from different genres will start to emulate one another's systems and become mixed-genre media. And just as the games become more similar, the people that make those games are expected to become more similar. This is where the tropes of hypermasculinity and antifeminism and anti-individualism start to become apparent. Dyer-Witheford & de Peuter in "'EA Spouse' and the Crisis of Video Game Labor" state that "for many, the initially enjoyable aspects of work in digital play mutate into a linchpin of exploitative and exclusionary practices, including exclusion based upon gender" (601).

Gender moderation is another aspect of production culture that contributes to the precarity of videogame production and perpetuation of negative tropes. Julie Prescott and Jan Bogg in "The Computer Games Industry" find that gender segregation is still happening in triple-A production spaces, and that women who do enter the industry must renegotiate their gender identity in order to fit in better with male coworkers (142). Robin Johnson, in "Technomasculinities and Its Influence in Videogame Production" (2018) outlines how, if they do not do the work of renegotiating, they run the risk of being accused of being "fake gamers" and have their passion called into question (254). This further demonstrates an unwillingness on the part of male production workers to accept alternate forms of passion to their own, alternate forms of people, and what those people are capable of.

The act of renegotiating gender in videogame production spaces becomes an act of subsistence rather than the more modern act of subversion that queer theory has attempted to recast it as. Jack Halberstam in *Queer Art of Failure* (2011) talks about failure as an iterative process where "failing" does not denote the end of an endeavor, but rather as a way of considering new methods to approach solving a problem (89). In modern culture, gender fluidity is recognized and is becoming more and more accepted, and people are free to express their gender how they see fit. Guattari, in *Soft Subversions* talks about how, within capitalist subjectivation, nonmale bodies, or bodies that are not willing to perform the necessary gender renegotiating to become-male become a hindrance. In an interview Johnson conducted in "Hiding in Plain Sight," he was able to extract a clear look at gender in the videogame production process: "other men offered a clearer window into the sexism of the digital play industry, explaining, for example, that 'girls' often do not have 'the right ideas' when it comes to games but that it 'looks good' for a developer to employ 'some girls'" (579). The necessity of women bodies to renegotiate their femininity, or to become-male, to be taken seriously and valued in the videogame production process presents a very troubling look at how gender is performed in these spaces, and how videogame production's workplace culture has come to recognize only one certain type of body as acceptably axiomatizable.

WHAT HAPPENS NEXT

Neither issue I have talked about in this conclusion has a clean "this is what happens next" answer, which falls in line with the rest of this book. This work is a work of "understanding" and a form of our (my?) own struggle with meaning-making. Meaning, this work cannot and is not about presenting hard-and-fast facts. I have presented an *understanding* of a possible theoretical avenue to pursue a better way of understanding how and why the shiny veneer of videogame production is so alluring and how the concept of "passion" has gotten incorporated and operationalized by capital generation. My understanding of how passion functions, based on my informants, my own passion, and research around passion, is not flat: it functions as a motivator, a subjectivator, a fishhook, an ever-present "if I just a little harder work harder, maybe I can . . . ," and a bridge between work and play. This is but one corner of a larger picture of the embodied experiences of each and every person in videogame production. Passion operates in vastly different ways for each of my informants, for me, and for the people about whom scholars that I have sourced in this book have written about.

Additionally, I want to make clear that I have presented an *understanding* of the possible contours, becomings, and agencements responsible for creating a proximity of the ethicoaestehtic socius in videogame production. The list I crafted that laid out problems and ontoethical solutions, and then the deeper dive I did into the issues of crunch-via-others'-passion and short-term-union-alternatives present cold compresses for a brown recluse bite. While a cold compress might be helpful to stop swelling or rapid venom spread, it does not address the problem underneath the surface, causing necrosis. But, like I said previously, the diligence I have done in this text has been done in the hope of creating solid ground to start to treat the necrosis that has already occurred. But, I believe that the diligence I have put forth does not just create ground for actioning the semantic concerns I have raised. That diligence will also go a long way to opening up new conversations within game studies and media studies for how we, as scholarly activists, might plug into labor organization in meaningful ways.

If we believe that the processual assemblage is in the embryonic stages of passing through the deterritorialized assemblage per O'Sullivan (2010), we are in the midst of two worlds colliding. This colliding takes place in the form of late-stage capitalism and the capitalist socius trying to carrion-bird the ethicoaesthetic socius to the point where the capitalist socius can sustain autopoiesis while actively hampering the ethicoaesthetic socius from actualizing. We see this in the form of formerly subversive material becoming monetizable; one of my favorite examples being Sid Vicious, the swastika shirt, and how the capitalist socius managed to allow for monetizability in such reprehensible symbology in such a clever way. For a bit of context: Sid Vicious, of Sex Pistols fame, and Siouxsie Sioux, of Siouxsieand the Banshees fame, were among the first punks to start wearing Swastika memorabilia to illicit shock from people on the streets. The general modus for punks at the time to affect change came in the form of shock-value: shock with clothing, with lyrics, with property damage, etc. But, as Steve Knopper notes in "Nazi Punks F**k Off: How Black Flag, Bad Brains, and More Took Back Their Scene from White Supremacists" (2018), suddenly, there was a flood of people wearing swastikas that were wearing them for far different reasons than Vicious and Sioux. Suddenly, you had a massive rise in Nazism in a subset of already disaffected, somewhat directionless youth, which contributed to the Nazification of west-coast punk that we still see pieces of today. In response to this rise in Nazism, The Dead Kennedys (1981) wrote the song *Nazi Punks Fuck Off* to address the rise in Nazism and to partially fix the problem that Vicious and Sioux started unintentionally. To an extent, this song's signification as a Nazi-hunting anthem did enough to dissuade most punks to drop Nazism, but even today there are echoes of that Nazism in certain areas of DIY/hardcore/punk music and culture that never quite went away. The same ideologies, rigor, cohesion, and direction that Nazism represented got transferred to other subsets of the culture, just without the *outright* anti-Semitism, racism, sexism, and homo/transphobia. For example, with the introduction of living a straightedge[5] lifestyle into DIY/hardcore/punk culture, "crews" started to form that sought to police venues/cities/scenes to dissuade smokers, drinkers, and sex-havers from being part of that scene. In effect, early "crews" were performing their own cultural eugenics, just without the swastika.

Fast-forward from the Dead Kennedys and 80s punk to mainstream culture in 2010. The same shirt that was meant to stoke a rebellion, but instead created a haven for Nazism, suddenly became actively commodifiable. The now-defunct memorabilia reseller Helen Hall was responsible for selling the original shirt, worn by Sid Vicious, made by made by Malcom McLaren, valued at $15,000 USD. The sale of this shirt caused an uproar, as would be expected. Who in their right mind would buy a shirt with a Swastika on it, especially in such close proximity to Jesse James's attempted sale of a replica Red Baron that, additionally, caused outrage? Though the buyer of the shirt was never identified, there were merch creators that took advantage of the shirt's rise to public interest to create their own lines of Swastika-related merch. They parroted facts about the original message of the shirt being an anti-Nazi tool similarly to Vicious and Sioux's, and similarly to the unintended rise of Nazism from them, these merch sellers started to see large sectors of White Supremacy groups buying the shirts. Obviously the merch sellers went on record as being anti-Semites and anti-Nazis, but capital is the great equalizer in regards to cultural ethics.

This is just one example of how the capitalist socius, given enough time, will coopt cultural markers and movements for its own autopoietic movements. Though possibly outside of the date range for the embryonic processual assemblage starting its journey through the deterritorialized assemblage, this is a prime example of the capitalist socius' ability to twist cultural markers, erase or bastardize historical points of contention, and create opportunistic and predatory capital generation opportunities: all for sustaining autopoiesis.

As I have said throughout this work, and as I am sure that I have shown (both intentionally and unintentionally), there are no clean lines of egress away from our current assemblage of videogame production to a more generative future. There are glimmers of hope, such as GWA, RJTV, and SNJV. There is a clear impetus in US videogame production to start to stand up to exploitative practices, which we see in the form of organized walkouts, organized protests, and the use of social media to provide a lens of truth that is not mediated by organizational communications. But, as with any discussion around the plane of immanence, assemblages, and rhizomatic logics, it is important to at least pay heed to the events happening outside of the immediate subject matter area. There are so many cultural, society, and ecological issues imbricated on top of the issues I have discussed that are daisy chaining out of, into, and around the issues present in videogame production. Any understandings that I have created through this work also have to be understood in context of those events, and in context of those assemblages. Though outside of the scope of this work, I do want to revisit a future book that I believe is prescient and necessary for *this* book to move forward in substantial ways. I firmly believe that there is a layer deeper than just simple affect that can be collocated alongside cruel optimism and passion in the form of dis/ability, mainly as another element of the capitalist socius' subjectivation stream in videogame production. Few other industries valorize bodily and affective harm the way that videogame production does, and I believe that that valorization and the tie-in to passion that those "battle scars" signal has a disabilities studies-relevant tie-in that could actually help shore up the problems I have talked about here.

It is so difficult to talk about, in a substantive way, the problems apparent in videogame production without paying attention to seemingly out of scope problems, such as dis/ability in videogame production, or environmental ethics in videogame production. Environmental destruction and cultural exploitation to create game systems are an often-overlooked part of the story when creating games hardware. In 2018, Rebekah Valentine wrote an expose around tech firms and human rights violations which found that a number of smelters and refiners in the pipeline for creating PlayStation 4s were not up to code with the Responsible Mineral Assurance Process, which puts in place rules and regulations for responsible mineral extraction and processing. Additionally, Sony bought from mines in "covered countries" such as the Democratic Republic of Congo and surrounding countries, which actively endorse the use of behavior that are considered human rights violations. Often times, these mines (and their associated smelters and refiners) run on child labor, violent coercion, and awful working conditions to extract the most value for the labor performed. Again, though out of the scope of this book, it is still imperative that these agencements be given equal understanding and critique as all other parts of the assemblage. Simply because they do not impact the immediacy of the problems I have outlined in this work does not mean that they do not have a direct impact. The capitalist socius is the imbrication point for a litany of these problems; systems of capital need readily exploitable work forces for *all parts* of a production process: the material, the immaterial, and the affective, hence why further work on the daisy chain effects of the socius are necessary to ensure that ontoethics and the processual assemblage can both grow and become the changes that we need.

NOTES

1. https://www.hollywoodreporter.com/news/general-news/riot-games-employees-stage-walkout-protest-companys-culture-1207713/.

2. https://www.polygon.com/23007018/activision-blizzard-workers-walkout-vaccine-mandate-dropped.

3. The King's Diversity Space Tool posts made by Blizzard live in two places: the first, accessible via the Internet Archive's Wayback Machine, talks about the diversity tool in terms of active use within Blizzard's development. After what can only be called an ocean of vitriolic feedback from academics, gamers, cultural critics, and even mainstream media sources, Blizzard edited the article to remove mentions of the tool's use in active development, and added an editor's note at the beginning saying that they had never used the tool in development. That version is the currently live version of the post, and can be found here.

4. For a comprehensive tracing of how Lara Croft's image started as a hypersexualized one and actually became one of empowerment, see Briana Wu's "From Sex Symbol to Icon: How Crystal Dynamics saved Lara Croft" (2015).

5. Straightedge refers to lifestyle choices made by those associated with punk/hardcore/DIY music where the person refrains from using alcohol, tobacco, or recreational drugs, even if legal (Haenfler, 2015). Some adherents take this to further mean abstaining from promiscuous sex, following a vegan diet, and not using caffeine or prescription drugs (Sutherland, 2006).

Bibliography

Ahmed, Sara. *On Being Included: Racism and Diversity in Institutional Life*. Durham: Duke University Press, 2012.

BAFTAGuru. "Peter Molyneux—'Show People You Are Enthusiastic And Passionate'." YouTube, 21 Aug, 2012. https://www.youtube.com/watch?v=dJFHo1lZe4I

Batchelor, James. "Activision Blizzard's Anti-Union Efforts Continue Ahead of Raven Vote." GamesIndustry.biz. GamesIndustry.biz, May 10, 2022. https://www.gamesindustry.biz/articles/2022–05–10-activision-blizzards-anti-union-efforts-continue-ahead-of-next-weeks-raven-vote.

Batchelor, James. "Rockstar Has Been 'Working 100-Hour Weeks' on Red Dead Redemption 2." GamesIndustry.biz, October 15, 2018. https://www.gamesindustry.biz/rockstar-has-been-working-100-hour-weeks-on-red-dead-redemption-2.

Baum, J. Robert, Edwin A. Locke, and Ken G. Smith. "A Multidimensional Model of Venture Growth." *Academy of Management Journal* 44, no. 2 (2001): 292–303. https://doi.org/10.5465/3069456.

Berlant, Lauren Gail. *Cruel Optimism*. Durham, NC: Duke University Press, 2012.

Blackman, Lisa, and Couze Venn. "Affect." *Body & Society* 16, no. 1 (2010): 8–28. https://doi.org/https://doi.org/10.1177/1357034X09354769.

Brennen, Bonnie. "Cultural Discourse of Journalists: The Material Conditions of Newsroom Labor." Essay. In *Newsworkers: Toward a History of the Rank and File*, edited by Bonnie Brennen and Hanno Hardt, 75–109. Minnesota: University of Minnesota Press, 1996.

Brooks, Frederick Phillips. *The Mythical Man-Month: Essays on Software Engineering*. Reading, MA: Addison-Wesley, 1974.

Bulut, Ergin. "Glamor Above, Precarity Below: Immaterial Labor in the Video Game Industry." *Critical Studies in Media Communication* 32, no. 3 (2015): 193–207. https://doi.org/10.1080/15295036.2015.1047880.

Bulut, Ergin. "Playboring in the Tester Pit." *Television & New Media* 16, no. 3 (2014): 240–58. https://doi.org/10.1177/1527476414525241.

Butler, Judith P. *Gender Trouble: Feminism and the Subversion of Identity*. New York: Routledge, 1990.

Butler, Judith. *Notes toward a Performative Theory of Assembly*. Cambridge, MA: Cambridge University Press, 2015.

Campbell, Colin. "The Game Industry's Disposable Workers." Polygon. Polygon, December 19, 2016. https://www.polygon.com/features/2016/12/19/13878484/ game-industry-worker-misclassification.

Chebotareva, Veronika. "Why Ukrainian CG Market Is One Of The Driving Forces Behind The Success Of Games Industry." Gamasutra, 2019. https://www .gamasutra.com/blogs/VeronikaChebotareva/20190404/340123/Why_Ukrainian _CG_Market_Is_One_Of_The_Driving_Forces_Behind_The_Success_Of_Games _Industry.php.

Chia, Aleena. "The Moral Calculus of Vocational Passion in Digital Gaming." *Television & New Media* 20, no. 8 (2019): 767–77. https://doi.org/10.1177 /1527476419851079.

Crowley, Martha, Daniel Tope, Lindsey Joyce Chamberlain, and Randy Hodson. "Neo-Taylorism at Work: Occupational Change in the Post-Fordist Era." *Social Problems* 57, no. 3 (2010): 421–47. https://doi.org/10.1525/sp.2010.57.3.421.

D'Anastasio, Cecilia. "Inside The Culture Of Sexism At Riot Games." Kotaku, 2018. https://kotaku.com/inside-the-culture-of-sexism-at-riot-games-1828165483.

D'Anastasio, Cecilia. "A Big Union Wants to Make Videogame Workers' Lives More Sane." Wired. Conde Nast, January 7, 2020. https://www.wired.com /story/big-union-make-videogame-workers-lives-sane/?fbclid=IwAR0SnUQV -4Qw2e0OnhewkuqDM0Z-K-VU32CqOV7MoFGhtQh-BUvVJzgwwgk.

Deleuze, Gilles, and Félix Guattari. *What Is Philosophy?* London.: Verso, 1994.

Deleuze, Gilles, and Félix Guattari. *A Thousand Plateaus*. Minneapolis: University of Minnesota Press, 1980.

Deleuze, Gilles, and Félix Guattari. *Anti-Oedipus: Capitalism and Schizophrenia*. Minneapolis: University of Minnesota Press, 1983.

Deuze, Mark. *Media Work*. Cambridge: Polity, 2007.

Deuze, Mark, Chase Bowen Martin, and Christian Allen. "The Professional Identity of Gameworkers." *Convergence: The International Journal of Research into New Media Technologies* 13, no. 4 (2007): 335–53. https://doi. org/10.1177/1354856507081947.

di Salvo, Betsy, C. Meadows, K. Perry, T. McKlin, and A. Bruckman. "ACM:Technical Symposium on Computer Science Education - SIGCSE '13." 44, n.d.

Dibbell, Julian. "Invisible Labor, Invisible Play: Online Gold Farming and the Boundary between Jobs and Games." *Vanderbilt Journal ofEntertainment & Technology Law* 18, no. 3 (2016): 419–65.

Duckworth, Angela, and Christopher Peterson, and Michael Matthews, and Dennis Kelly. (2007). "Grit: Perseverance and Passion for Long-Term Goals." *Journal of Personality and Social Psychology*. 92. 1087–101. 10.1037/0022–3514.92.6.1087.

Dyer-Witheford, Nick. "The Political Economy of Canada's Video and Computer Game Industry." *Canadian Journal of Communication* 30, no. 2 (2005): 187–210. https://doi.org/10.22230/cjc.2005v30n2a1575.

Dyer-Witheford, Nick, and Greig De Peuter. *Games of Empire: Global Capitalism and Video Games*. Minneapolis: University of Minnesota Press, 2009.

Dyer-Witheford, Nick, and Greig S. De Peuter. "'EA Spouse' and the Crisis of Video Game Labor: Enjoyment, Exclusion, Exploitation, and Exodus." *Canadian Journal of Communication* 31, no. 3 (2006). https://doi.org/10.22230/cjc.2006v31n3a1771.

Dyer-Witheford, Nick, and Zena Sharman. "The Political Economy of Canada's Video and Computer Game Industry." *Canadian Journal of Communication* 30, no. 2 (2005): 187–210. https://doi.org/10.22230/cjc.2005v30n2a1575.

Farokhmanesh, Megan. "ArenaNet Firings Cast a Chilling Shadow across the Game Industry." *The Verge* July 12, 2018. https://www.theverge.com/2018/7/12/17565218/arenanet-guild-wars-firing-games-social-media-harassment.

Fernandez, Marisa, and Sara Fischer. "More than 30 Media Companies Have Unionized in the Past 2 Years." Axios, 2019. https://www.axios.com/media-talent-strikes-back-union-writers-guild-hollywood-86b24f65-6d5f-4e1a-9f83-cc09a405d28d.html.

Fisher, Howard. "Sexy, Dangerous—and Ignored." *Games and Culutre* 10, no. 6 (2015).

Fisher, Stephanie, and Alison Harvey. "Intervention for Inclusivity: Gender Politics and Indie Game Development." *Loading . . . The Journal of the Canadian Game Studies Association* 7, no. 11 (2013).

Flanagan, Mary, and Helen Nissenbaum. *Values at Play in Digital Games*. Cambridge, MA: The MIT Press, 2016.

Foucault, Michel. *The History of Sexuality*. London: Penguin Books, 1990.

Gach, Ethan. "Inside Blizzard Developers' Infamous Bill 'Cosby Suite.'" Kotaku, July 28, 2021. https://kotaku.com/inside-blizzard-developers-infamous-bill-cosby-suite-1847378762.

Gallagher, Rob, Carolyn Jong, and Kalervo Sinervo. "Who Wrote the Elder Scrolls?: Modders, Developers, and the Mythology of Bethesda Softworks." *Loading . . .* 10, no. 16 (2017).

Game Workers Unite!, 2018. https://www.gameworkersunite.org/about-us.

Game Informer. "How Skyrim's Director Todd Howard Got Into The Industry." 29 Nov., 2011. https://www.youtube.com/watch?v=xoYDjzGN44Y

Giddens, Anthony. *The Constitution of Society: Outline of the Theory of Structuration*. Cambridge: Polity, 1984.

Grant, Christopher. "Joystiq Interview: Epic's Mike Capps Responds to Accusations of 'Exploitative' Working Conditions." Engadget, 2009. https://www.engadget.com/2009/04/22/joystiq-interview-epics-michael-capps-responds-to-accusations/.

Griffith, Alison I., and Dorothy E. Smith. *Mothering for Schooling*. New York: RoutledgeFalmer, 2005.

Grosz, Elizabeth. *Chaos, Territory, Art: Deleuze and the Framing of the Earth*. Columbia University Press, 2008.

Grosz, Elizabeth. *The Incorporeal: Ontology, Ethics, and the Limits of Materialism*. New York: Columbia University Press, 2017.

Grosz, Elizabeth. *Volatile Bodies*. Routledge, 1994.

Guattari, Félix, and Lotringer Sylvère. *Soft Subversions*. Semiotext(e), 1996.

Guattari, Félix, and Nadaud Stéphane. *The Anti-Œdipus Papers*. New York, NY: Semiotext(e), 2006.

Guattari, Félix, and Nadaud Stéphane. *The Anti-Œdipus Papers*. New York, NY: Semiotext(e), 2006.

Guattari, Félix. *Chaosmosis: An Ethico-Aesthetic Paradigm*. Sydney: Power Publications, 1995.

Guattari, Félix. *The Three Ecologies*. Bloomsbury, 1989.

Guattari Félix, and Nadaud Stéphane. *The Anti-Œdipus Papers*. New York, NY: Semiotext(e), 2006.

Hacker, Sally L. "Sex Stratification, Technology and Organizational Change: A Longitudinal Case Study of AT&T." *Social Problems* 26, no. 5 (1979): 539–57. https://doi.org/10.1525/sp.1979.26.5.03a00060.

Hacker, Sally L. "The Culture of Engineering: Woman, Workplace and Machine." *Women's Studies International Quarterly* 4, no. 3 (1981): 341–53. https://doi.org /10.1016/s0148-0685(81)96559-3.

Haenfler, Ross. "Punk Rock, Hardcore and Globalization." *The SAGE Handbook of Popular Music*, 2015, 278–96. https://doi.org/10.4135/9781473910362.n16.

Halberstam, Jack. *The Queer Art of Failure*. Duke University Press, 2011.

Han, Clara. "Precarity, Precariousness, and Vulnerability." *Annual Review of Anthropology* 47, no. 1 (2018): 331–43. https://doi.org/10.1146/annurev-anthro -102116-041644.

Hardt, Hanno, Bonnie Brennen, and Bonnie Brennen. "Cultural Discourse of Journalists: The Material Conditions of Newsroom Labor." Essay. In *Newsworkers: Toward a History of the Rank and File*, 75–110. University of Minnesota Press, 1996.

Hardt, Michael, and Antonio Negri. *Assembly*. New York: Oxford University Press, 2019.

Hardt, Michael, and Antonio Negri. *Empire*. Cambridge, MA: Harvard University Press, 2000.

Hern, Alex. "Twitch to Ban Users from Streaming Unlicensed Gambling Content." *The Guardian*, September 21, 2022. https://www.theguardian.com/games/2022/ sep/21/twitch-to-ban-users-from-streaming-unlicensed-gambling-content.

Hyman, Paul. "OUTSOURCING: Video Game Art Is Increasingly 'To Go.'" *Game Developer* 15, no. 8 (2008).

Isbister, Katherine. *How Games Move Us: Emotion by Design*. MIT Press, 2017.

Jarvis, Jeff. "The Future of News Is Entrepreneurial." BuzzMachine, November 2, 2009. https://buzzmachine.com/2009/11/01/the-future-of-journalism-is -entrepreneurial/.

Johnson (a), Robin. "Hiding in Plain Sight: Reproducing Masculine Culture at a Video Game Studio." *Communication, Culture & Critique* 7, no. 4 (2013): 578–94. https://doi.org/10.1111/cccr.12023.

Johnson (b), Robin. "Toward Greater Production Diversity." *Games and Culture* 8, no. 3 (2013): 136–60. https://doi.org/10.1177/1555412013481848.

Johnson, Robin. "Technomasculinity and Its Influence in Video Game Production." Essay. In *Masculinities in Play*, edited by Gerald A. Voorhees and Nicholas Taylor, 249–62. Palgrave Macmillan, 2018.

Kerr, Aphra, and John D. Kelleher. "The Recruitment of Passion and Community in the Service of Capital: Community Managers in the Digital Games Industry." *Critical Studies in Media Communication* 32, no. 3 (2015): 177–92. https://doi.org /10.1080/15295036.2015.1045005.

Kim, Matt. "IGDA Director Says Capital, Not Unions, Will Keep Game Development Jobs Secure." USgamer.net. USGamer.net, March 19, 2018. https://www.usgamer .net/articles/igda-director-union-crunch-interview.

Kuchlich, Julian. "Precarious Playbour: Modders and the Digital Games Industry." *The Fibreculture Journal* 5 (2005).

Kunzelman, Cameron. "Crunch Culture Is Never Just About Individual Choice." Waypoint. VICE, August 23, 2017. https://waypoint.vice.com/en_us/article/kzznee /crunch-culture-is-never-just-about-individual-choice.

Landa, Manuel De. *Intensive Science and Virtual Philosophy*. London: Bloomsbury, 2002.

Latour, Bruno. "How to Talk About the Body? The Normative Dimension of Science Studies." *Body & Society* 10, no. 2–3 (2004): 205–29. https://doi.org/10.1177 /1357034x04042943.

Lauteria, Evan. "Ga(y)Mer Theory: Queer Modding as Resistance." *Reconstruction* 12, no. 2 (2012).

Lazzarato, M. 1996. "Immaterial Labor," trans. P. Colilli and E. Emery, in M. Hardt and P. Virno (eds.) *Radical Thought in Italy: A Potential Politics*. Minneapolis and London: University of Minnesota Press, 133–147.

Lazzarato, Maurizio. *Signs and Machines: Capitalism and the Production of Subjectivity*. Los Angeles, CA: Semiotext(e), 2014.

Leab, Daniel Josef. *A Union of Individuals: the Formation of the American Newspaper Guild, 1933–1936*. University Microfilms International, 1970.

Legault, Marie-Josée, and Johanna Weststar. "The Capacity for Mobilization in Project-Based Cultural Work: A Case of the Video Game Industry." *Canadian Journal of Communication* 40, no. 2 (2015). https://doi.org/10.22230/cjc .2015v40n2a2805.

Llerena, Patrick, et al. "Division of Labor and Division of Knowledge: A Case Study of Innovation in the Video Game Industry." Schumpeterian Perspectives on Innovation, Competition and Growth, 2009, pp. 315–333., doi:10.1007/978-3–540–93777–7_18.

Marx, Karl. *Grundrisse*. London: Macmillan, 1858.

Moore, Phoebe V. *The Quantified Self in Precarity*. London: Routledge, 2017.

Morrison, Joshua T. "Reveling in Uselessness: Queer and Trans Media, Consumptive labor, and Cultural Capital." Dissertation, ProQuest Dissertations & Theses, 2019.

Mosher, Donald L., and Mark Sirkin. "Measuring a Macho Personality Constellation." *Journal of Research in Personality* 18, no. 2 (1984): 150–63. https://doi.org/10 .1016/0092–6566(84)90026–6.

Mosher, Donald L., and Mark Sirkin. "Measuring a Macho Personality Constellation." *Journal of Research in Personality* 18, no. 2 (1984): 150–63. https://doi.org/10 .1016/0092–6566(84)90026–6.

Mosher, Donald L., and Silvan S. Tomkins. "Scripting the Macho Man: Hypermasculine Socialization and Enculturation." *Journal of Sex Research* 25, no. 1 (1988): 60–84. https://doi.org/10.1080/00224498809551445.

Muñoz, José. *Disidentifications: Queers of Color and the Performance of Politics.* University of Minnesota Press, 1999.

Murnieks, Charles Y., Elaine Mosakowski, and Melissa S. Cardon. "Pathways of Passion." *Journal of Management* 40, no. 6 (2012): 1583–1606. https://doi.org/10.1177/0149206311433855.

Neilson, Brett, and Ned Rossiter. "From Precarity to Precariousness and Back Again: Labor, Life and Unstable Networks." *The Fibreculture Journal* 5 (2005).

Ngai, Sianne. *Ugly Feelings.* Cambridge, MA: Harvard University Press, 2007.

Nickell, Doug, Jana Kliestikova, and Mara Kovacova. "The Increasing Casualization of the Gig Economy: Insecure Forms of Work, Precarious Employment Relationships, and the Algorithmic Management of Labor." *Psychosociological Issues in Human Resource Management* 7, no. 1 (2019). https://doi.org/10.22381/PIHRM7120197.

Nietzsche, Friedrich Wilhelm, Thomas Common, Paul V. Cohn, and Maude Dominica Petre. *The Gay Science.* Mineola, NY: Dover Publications, Inc., 1882.

Nietzsche, Friedrich Wilhelm. *Thus Spoke Zarathustra.* Edinburgh: Foulis, 1883.

O'Sullivan, Simon. "Guattari's Aesthetic Paradigm: From the Folding of the Finite/Infinite Relation to Schizoanalytic Metamodelisation." *Deleuze Studies* 4, no. 2 (2010): 256–86. https://doi.org/10.3366/dls.2010.0006.

Paaßen, Benjamin, Thekla Morgenroth, and Michelle Stratemeyer. "What Is a True Gamer? The Male Gamer Stereotype and the Marginalization of Women in Video Game Culture." *Sex Roles* 76, no. 7–8 (2016): 421–35. https://doi.org/10.1007/s11199-016-0678-y.

Parker, Felan, Jennifer R. Whitson, and Bart Simon. "Megabooth: The Cultural Intermediation of Indie Games." *New Media & Society* 20, no. 5 (2017): 1953–72. https://doi.org/10.1177/1461444817711403.

Paul, Christopher A. *The Toxic Meritocracy of Video Games: Why Gaming Culture Is the Worst.* Minneapolis: University of Minnesota Press, 2018.

Peticca-Harris, Amanda, Johanna Weststar, and Steve Mckenna. "The Perils of Project-Based Work: Attempting Resistance to Extreme Work Practices in Video Game Development." *Organization* 22, no. 4 (2015): 570–87. https://doi.org/10.1177/1350508415572509.

Prescott, Julie, and Jan Bogg. "The Computer Games Industry." In *Women in Engineering, Science and Technology: Education and Career Challenges*, 138–58. Aileen Cater-Steel and Emily Cater, Engineering Science Reference, 2010.

Reider, David, and Matthew Halm. "Touch-Interactive Rhetorics: Everting the Real through Wonder and Movement." Essay. In *Re-Programmable Rhetorics*, edited by Steven Holmes and Michael Farris. Utah Valley State UP, 2022.

Resch, Robert Paul. *Althusser and the Renewal of Marxist Social Theory.* Berkeley, Cal.: University of California Press, 1992.

Rusch, Doris C. *Making Deep Games: Designing Games with Meaning and Purpose.* CRC Press, Taylor & Francis Group, 2017.

Salter, Anastasia, and Bridget Blodgett. "Hypermasculinity & Dickwolves: The Contentious Role of Women in the New Gaming Public." *Journal of Broadcasting & Electronic Media* 56, no. 3 (2012): 401–16. https://doi.org/10.1080/08838151.2012.705199.

Schreier, Jason. "The Horrible World Of Video Game Crunch." Kotaku. kotaku.com, September 26, 2016. https://kotaku.com/crunch-time-why-game-developers-work-such-insane-hours-1704744577.

Schrier, Jason. "Why Game Developers Keep Getting Laid Off." Kotaku, 2014. https://kotaku.com/why-game-developers-keep-getting-laid-off-1583192249.

Siapera, Euginia. "Affective Labor and Media Work." Essay. In *Making Media: Production, Practices, and Professions*, edited by Mark Deuze. Amsterdam: Amsterdam University Press, 2019.

Sims, Christo. *Disruptive Fixation: School Reform and the Pitfalls of Techno-Idealism*. Princeton University Press, 2017.

Sotamaa, Olli. "On Modder Labor, Commodification of Play, and Mod Competitions." *First Monday* 12, no. 9 (2007). https://doi.org/10.5210/fm.v12i9.2006.

Spangler, Todd. "YouTube Star Toby 'Tobuscus' Turner Responds to Sexual-Assault Allegations." *Variety* April 11, 2016. https://variety.com/2016/digital/news/toby-turner-tobuscus-sexual-assault-allegations-1201750607/.

Spinuzzi, Clay. *All Edge: Inside the New Workplace Networks*. University of Chicago Press, 2015.

Steinkuehler, Constance. "The Mangle of Play." *Games and Culture* 1, no. 3 (2006): 199–213. https://doi.org/10.1177/1555412006290440.

"STJV." Version française. Le Syndicat des Travailleurs et Travailleuses du Jeu Vidéo, 2018. https://www.stjv.fr/en/.

Sutherland, Sam. "Straight Edge Punk the Complicated Contradictions of Straight Edge Punk." *Exclaim!*, July 1, 2006. https://exclaim.ca/music/article/straight_edge_punk-complicated_contradictions_of_straight.

Taylor, James R., and Elizabeth Van Every. *The Emergent Organization: Communication as Its Site and Surface*. Psychology Press, 2008.

Taylor, Nicholas. "Cheerleaders/Booth Babes/ Halo Hoes: pro-Gaming, Gender and Jobs for the Boys." *Digital Creativity* 20, no. 4 (2009): 239–52. https://doi.org/10.1080/14626260903290323.

Taylor, Nicholas, Jen Jenson, and Suzanne De Castell. "Cheerleaders/Booth Babes/ Halo Hoes: pro-Gaming, Gender and Jobs for the Boys." *Digital Creativity* 20, no. 4 (2009): 239–52. https://doi.org/10.1080/14626260903290323.

Thorgren, Sara, and Joakim Wincent. "Passion and Challenging Goals: Drawbacks of Rushing into Goal-Setting Processes." *Journal of Applied Social Psychology* 43, no. 11 (2013): 2318–29. https://doi.org/10.1111/jasp.12181.

Tokumitsu, Miya. *Do What You Love and Other Lies about Success & Happiness*. Regan Arts, 2015.

Tokumitsu, Miya. "In the Name of Love." *Jacobin*, 2014. https://www.jacobinmag.com/2014/01/in-the-name-of-love/.

Valentine, Rebekah. "ESA Reportedly Troubled by Eroded Trust, Harsh Management Styles." GamesIndustry.biz, May 10, 2019. https://www.gamesindustry.biz/esa -reportedly-troubled-by-eroding-trust-challenging-management-styles.

Varela, Francisco, and Humberto Maturana. "Mechanism and Biological Explanation." *Philosophy of Science* 39, no. 3 (1972): 378–82. https://doi.org/10.1086/288458.

Visweswaran, Kamala. *Fictions of Feminist Ethnography*. Minneapolis: University of Minnesota Press, 1994.

Walsh, Paul. "Precarity." *ELT Journal* 73, no. 4 (2019): 459–62. https://doi. org/10.1093/elt/ccz029.

Weber, Max. *Weber: Political Writings*. Edited by Peter Lassman. Translated by Ronald Speirs. *Cambridge Texts in the History of Political Thought*. Cambridge: Cambridge University Press, 1994. doi:10.1017/CBO9780511841095.

Weber, Max. *The Protestant Ethic and the Spirit of Capitalism*. New York, NY: Scribner's Sons, 1958.

Weber, Max. *The Methodology of the Social Sciences*. Translated by Edward Shils. New York: Free Press, 1904/1949.

Webster, Andrew. "Rockstar Clarifies Red Dead Redemption 2's '100-Hour Work Week,' Following Backlash." *The Verge* October 15, 2018. https://www.theverge .com/2018/10/15/17979606/rockstar-red-dead-redemption-2-crunch-100-hour -work-week.

Weststar, Johanna, and Marie-Josée Legault. "Why Might a Videogame Developer Join a Union?" *Labor Studies Journal* 42, no. 4 (2017): 295–321. https://doi.org /10.1177/0160449x17731878.

Weststar, Johanna, Victoria O'Meara, and Marie-Josee Legault. Rep. *Developer Satisfaction Survey 2017: Summary Report*. International Game Developers Association, 2017.

Whyman, Tom. "Beware of Cupcake Fascism | Tom Whyman." *The Guardian*, April 8, 2014. https://www.theguardian.com/commentisfree/2014/apr/08/ beware-of-cupcake-fascism.

Wilkins, Lee, and Bonnie Brennen. "Conflicted Interests, Contested Terrain: Journalism Ethics Codes Then and Now." *Journalism Studies* 5, no. 3 (2004): 297–309. https://doi.org/10.1080/1461670042000246061.

Williams, Ian. "After Destroying Lives For Decades, Gaming Is Finally Talking Unionization." Waypoint. VICE, March 23, 2018. https://waypoint.vice.com/ en_us/article/7xdv5e/after-destroying-lives-for-decades-gaming-is-finally-talking -unionization.

Williams, Ian. "'You Can Sleep Here All Night': Video Games and Labor." *Jacobin*, 2013. http://www.jacobinmag.com/2013/11/video-game-industry/.

Wilson, Julie A. *Neoliberalism*. New York: Routledge, 2018.

Woodcock, Jamie, and Mark Johnson. "The Affective labor and Performance of Live Streaming on Twitch.TV." *Television and New Media* 20, no. 8 (2019): 813–23.

Wu, Brianna. "From Sex Symbol to Icon: How Crystal Dynamics Saved Lara Croft." Polygon. Polygon, November 11, 2015. https://www.polygon.com/2015/11/11 /9712168/tomb-raider-lara-croft-sex-symbol-icon.

Index

138   *Index*

About the Author

Dr. Joshua Jackson is a Computer Games Modeling and Animation lecturer at the University of Derby. He grew up in Dallas, Texas, moved around the country for university, and transitioned to the UK higher education system because of its proximity to, and rich history of, unions and collective action. Joshua's research centers on videogame production labor, queerness in technologized spaces, and seeking new ways and means of creating digital tapestries of stories from queer and marginal bodies. In the immediacy, Joshua's research seeks to help renegotiate how labor, capital, and passion are articulated in order to assist immaterial laborers in taking concrete, material action for better working conditions. Outside of research, Joshua enjoys traveling, learning about food that is entwined with the cultures of the places he visits, and cats in all shapes and sizes. He volunteers at a cat rescue in the East Midlands.